The Simple Road Toward
Financial Freedom

The Simple Road Toward Financial Freedom
A Guide to Building Wealth and Independence

Mark Schlipman and Steve Short

All material contained herein is copyrighted by Simple Road, LLC
2265 Bagnell Dam Blvd. Suite 200 Lake Ozark, MO 65049
(This address is not registered or affiliated with Cetera Advisor Networks, LLC)

Published by Game Changer Publishing
Cover Credits: Skylar Cawley

Hardcover ISBN: 978-1-962656-44-3
Digital: ISBN: 978-1-962656-46-7

www.GameChangerPublishing.com

DEDICATION

To our loving wives for being very supportive and putting up with us running with this crazy book idea for the last 2+ years. Also, thanks to our kids for clearly communicating with us; this information is very valuable and needed for their age group, and, unfortunately, it's not something they learned in school.

Thank you for reading our book!

As a token of our appreciation, we would like to offer you a free gift we are confident will be helpful on your journey toward financial freedom.

Please visit: www.simpleroadbook.com/gift
Or
Simply Scan the QR Code Here:

The Simple Road Toward
Financial Freedom

A Guide to Building Wealth and Independence

Mark Schlipman & Steve Short

www.GameChangerPublishing.com

Foreword

Hello readers! You might be wondering why I'm writing the foreword to this book. It's a great question. One of the reasons is that I've known one of the authors, Steve Short, for over 35 years. Steve and I have had a great friendship, and I've watched him go on to have an amazingly successful career in business.

The other guy Mark… I met once. Seemed like a nice guy, but who knows??? It doesn't matter. What matters is these guys wrote a fantastic book! And I'm sure it was more Mark's idea than Steve's.

Yes, the title is *The Simple Road Toward Financial Freedom,* but this book is really more a guide to financial security. I love that the central idea is delayed gratification, which is something we talk a lot about with our own kids. Steve and Mark lay out the basic blocking and tackling (football reference) of putting a share of your earnings aside so that when you are ready to retire or even make a career change, you will be on solid financial footing.

I've been extremely fortunate in my career with finding the right people to guide me financially. However, had I been on my own, I would have been lost, and this is where this book can help you. These guys teach you how to take control of your life without living paycheck to paycheck. It's also a great read. I read it in 4 minutes, but I'm a graduate of the Evelyn Wood Speed Reading School.

Another great reason to buy this book is that a portion from every book sold is going to the charity Cancer for College, which provides need-based college scholarships to cancer survivors and amputees… you know what? I think I like Mark after all. This is a charity that I've been involved with for 30 years, and it is near and dear to our hearts.

Thanks for reading, and enjoy the book. If you run into me after making your first million, buy me dinner, please. I need it.

Will Ferrell

Table of Contents

The Climb

"If you can't explain it simply, you don't understand it well enough." – Albert Einstein

Most people would consider Forrest Gump to be a pretty simple guy. But despite a modest IQ of just 75, he has an uncanny knack for making the complex incredibly simple to understand. Even if you haven't seen the movie, you've probably come across his famous quote, "Life is like a box of chocolates. You never know what you're going to get." Forrest's observation from an Alabama bus bench wasn't just his major thesis on life. This clever one-liner also applies to the mindset of the average American investor. All too often, they work hard for forty years, only to be surprised at how little of their money is left over when they retire. To them, the financial system feels like a gamble. The stock market looks like a jumble of complicated acronyms and random numbers, no different from the blur of flashing lights and colors on a Las Vegas casino floor. No matter how hard they try to manage their finances—*they never know what they are going to get.*

Most people know they *should* save money for retirement and that they *should* invest, but at the end of the day, they don't take the simple actions to learn what they need to do to get there. They just hope that one day they'll open up the box of chocolates, and everything will have magically fallen into place.

1

They rely on luck instead of learning what steps to take to create financial freedom for themselves. They buy and sell stocks based on emotion rather than proven financial wisdom and often have no retirement plan in place.

The average consumer is just enjoying eating the chocolates in the box—one by one—spending their hard-earned paychecks just as quickly as they deposit them. As a result, they keep living paycheck to paycheck, year after year, hoping that one day they will get that big inheritance, big promotion, or big raise. Sadly, as soon as they get that windfall of cash, it usually evaporates just as quickly as they received it because they never had someone to teach them how to manage their money properly.

Many people think that being a millionaire is just a fantasy. If you polled strangers on the street and asked them what they would need to do to be a millionaire, they'd likely tell you that they would have to be a professional athlete, rob a bank, or become a movie star to rake in that kind of life-changing dough. Very few of them are aware of the reality that for most Americans, saving as little as 20% of their annual income and investing it in the right places could net them a million dollars in only 20-25 years.[1] Sadly, there is a large percentage of Americans who aren't financially literate. Only 57% of Americans claim to be financially literate, leaving the other 43% clueless.[2] We aren't just talking about 25-year-olds, either. Many people in their forties and fifties are still struggling to understand the complexities and nuances of how money works.

Returning to our fictional financial forecaster, Forrest Gump, a fun fact is that his character invested nearly $100k in a little startup called Apple Computers.

---

[1]This example is hypothetical only, and does not represent the actual performance of any particular investments. Investments in securities do not offer a fixed rate of return. Principal, yield and/or share price will fluctuate with changes in market conditions and when sold or redeemed, you may receive more or less than originally invested.

[2] https://www.cnbc.com/video/2022/04/08/financial-literacy-in-america.html. Author: Emily Lorsch, *This is Why Americans Can't Manage Their Money*, 4/8/22.

His imaginary investment in Apple stock back in 1994 would be worth tens of *billions* of dollars today![3] Despite being an average, simple guy, that one simple decision earned him a spot on Forbes 2012 Fictional 15[4] of the wealthiest fictional characters, alongside other magnates like Scrooge McDuck and Bruce Wayne (Batman). But you don't have to invest in the next big "fruit company" like Forrest did to become a millionaire.

If you're a little skeptical right now, don't worry. *You're* the reason we wrote this book. The best-kept secret in the financial industry is that understanding how to manage your money isn't some great mystery. It's a combination of simple concepts and simple actions that we are going to teach you.

Defining Your Financial Freedom

It is important to determine what defines financial freedom for you. Many people we talk with define financial freedom as acquiring **a million dollars**. We will be referencing the goal of acquiring a million dollars; however, your goal may be a different number, reducing debt, selling your business and/or another specific goal. Financial freedom for some people means having assets and a mindset that affords us a life we desire for ourselves and our families.

It Doesn't Have to Be So Hard

We know what you're probably thinking: *being a millionaire isn't easy*. But what if someone came along and told you that becoming a millionaire was actually simpler than you might think? Sure, it may be a lot of money, but with the right plan, it's not that complex. The goal behind this book is to

---

[3] This example is hypothetical only, and does not represent the actual performance of any particular investments. Investments in securities do not offer a fixed rate of return. Principal, yield and/or share price will fluctuate with changes in market conditions and when sold or redeemed, you may receive more or less than originally invested.

[4] https://www.forbes.com/special-report/2012/fictional-15-12/forrest-gump.html. Author: Michael Noer and David M. Ewalt, *The Forbes Fictional 15*, 4/23/12.

demystify some of the inner workings of the financial system to show you just how straightforward it can be to join the million-dollar club.

Metaphors can be valuable tools because they help us think about colossal concepts in simple ways. To use a metaphor, becoming a millionaire is a lot like climbing a mountain—it's a big concept. When you are standing on the ground looking up at the side of the mountain, it's easy to see the peak bursting out of the horizon. The goal is a million dollars by the time you reach the top. That's easy to see from the ground. But what you can't see right now are the cliff faces, hidden crags, and pathways that will lead you there. That's where we come in.

This book will be your guide. It will show you the simple road you need to follow to get to the top of the financial mountain. A mountain is a great visual aid for thinking about your financial journey because the goal of climbing a mountain is pretty self-explanatory—you want to make it up to the top. Even if you've never climbed a mountain before, intuitively, you know that it is not always easy and it's not a fast process. Becoming a millionaire is very similar. It will take commitment, hard work, and putting one foot in front of the other to follow the simple advice we will lay out in this book. In the chapters ahead, we will reference the mountain metaphor to help put your financial journey into perspective.

This journey will take consistent hard work, training, tools, and a game plan to scale the summit, but if you know what to do, **it is very possible for the average American**. You just need someone who has done it before to show you (and it also helps if they've successfully helped thousands of others with their investments.)

People don't *accidentally* climb 14,000-foot-tall mountains. Likewise, most people don't *accidentally* become millionaires. There is a simple strategy that you must follow to get there.

Preparing for the Climb

You can try to become a millionaire all by yourself, but just like climbing a mountain, it is nearly impossible without some support. Everyone needs a good guide. Even millionaires like professional quarterbacks make risky investments that lose them millions of dollars—we, of course, won't name any names. There are countless stories of people who amassed real wealth only to fall off the mountain and lose it all because they didn't have the right people in their corner guiding them.

We've divided the information in this book into three sections: *New to the Workforce, When Life Gets More Complicated, and Late-in-the-Game.* Breaking the chapters into three different sections allows you to easily find the information that is most useful to you and your current financial situation. It also gives you a preview of what's to come and some helpful considerations you should think about early in life to prepare for your later years. However, even though all the chapters in this book may not apply to you right now, we strongly encourage you to read the entire book because the information and knowledge it contains can help you at every stage of your financial climb.

To make it easy to get started, we've written this book to be a practical guide covering most of the basics of your financial future. This book will not go into depth on every aspect of financial planning, as many of the topics we will discuss could take an entire book just to explain. Remember, learning about investment strategies and money management is a *lifelong* process. Our goal is to help you get on the road to becoming a lifelong learner and understand the basics behind financial freedom. This book can't teach you everything there is to know. It is simply a guide that will provide real-world advice on how to help the process of becoming a millionaire.

In this book, just like mountain climbing, we will share things you need to look out for, what to avoid, and how you can prepare for the road ahead. If this sounds difficult, don't worry. You don't need to be a financial advisor to understand the knowledge and information contained in this book. The goal is to empower you, not make it so complicated that you need to hire a financial professional to interpret it for you. We will make this information as simple to understand as possible so that you don't waste any time getting on *The Simple Road Toward Financial Freedom*.

Why We Wrote This Book

Good things happen when two people from different backgrounds combine their skills in the pursuit of a common goal. We realized that combining forces could be really helpful for explaining the full picture behind financial planning. There are countless books written by financial advisors and money-savvy consumers alike. But when a financial advisor and a corporate executive combine their knowledge, it enhances the narrative. It also allows Mark Schlipman's skill sets as a financial advisor to complement Steve Short's consumer-side experience. From a practical how-to perspective, both authors have a lot to offer, and the goal is to make this information easy to understand and even easier to apply to your life.

Mark will share the latest in financial best practices that he uses to advise his clients on how to manage their portfolios. Mark's work as a financial advisor (owning multiple financial planning and wealth management offices across the Midwest) positions him as a financial professional with a passion for educating consumers on financial literacy. As an Accredited Investment Fiduciary, Mark is in the trenches with the consumer, and he has seen time and time again where financial advisors make simple concepts incredibly complicated. Mark's mission is to encourage readers that it doesn't need to be so hard. His biggest passion is his experience helping everyday people find the road toward financial freedom.

Meanwhile, Steve has always been told by supervisors and his employees that he has a real knack for breaking things down into their simplest form to make big concepts easy to understand. Steve's interest in investing began when he was a young boy stuck at his grandparent's house. Bored, back in the days before cable television, he picked up a copy of his grandfather's *Value Line* newsletter, a publication that wrote about individual stocks. After his grandfather explained the stock market in its simplest form, Steve began taking money from his after-school jobs and started buying small amounts of individual stocks of companies that he recognized and *Value Line* suggested might perform well. This early interest led him to almost pursue a career in finance. Instead, he took the corporate route, where he ended up putting his financial prowess to work, managing ultra-successful multibillion-dollar B2B and B2C divisions throughout the travel, technology, insurance, legal and retail industries.

Over dinner and drinks on September 21, 2021 (two hours before a Rolling Stones concert), we committed to writing this book and sharing *The Simple Road Toward Financial Freedom* with others. We have had countless conversations about the need for more financial literacy, especially for the younger generation. Steve saw this firsthand after his oldest children and their friends entered the workforce with minimal understanding of many of these concepts despite their college degrees.

Our ultimate goal for writing this book is to instill simple financial concepts for someone new to the workforce to get on *The Simple Road Toward Financial Freedom.*

Our approach is "simple" for two reasons:
1. We think you'll agree the concepts we've laid out are simple to follow.
2. Because you could potentially become a millionaire by simply contributing roughly 25% to 30% ($250k to $300k) of the funds yourself.[5]

---

[5] This example is hypothetical only, and does not represent the actual performance of any particular investments. Investments in securities do not offer a fixed rate of return. Principal, yield and/or share price will fluctuate with changes in market conditions and when sold or redeemed, you may receive more or less than originally invested.

That's not a typo. This book will show you how that's possible.

Most people don't realize they don't need to actually earn and save a million dollars to become a millionaire.

That's the difficult road. Our pathway is focused on getting you to the top of the mountain much faster, where "free money" makes up the other 70% to 75%. In our world, "free money" consists of stock market growth and company retirement plan contributions.

But even if you are further along on the trail, meaning you've been working for a while, many of these concepts and wealth-building strategies may be new to you. No matter where you are on the trail, we encourage you to read through this book from start to summit; you can still benefit from the information in the earlier chapters.

While many finance books are designed to be part of a sales funnel to sell you on hiring the author as a financial advisor, this book isn't designed to sell you anything. The goal is to help you get on the road toward financial freedom. Plain and simple. No matter where you are on your road toward financial freedom, we want you to know that *it's never too late to get started.*

PART 1

New To the Workforce

Starting the Climb: Mark's Journey

"It was pitch-black at the foot of the mountain. My mind was racing as adrenaline coursed through my veins at the thought of what I was about to put myself through. My knees felt wobbly, still tired from the lack of sleep the night before. All ten toes gripped the sole of my hiking boots as each fresh assault of the icy wind felt like a million sharp needles jabbing into my exposed, bare skin. My face, neckline, and hands all became numb in a matter of minutes. Cupping my hands to my face for warmth, I quickly regained control over my mental state. Calming my mind, I shifted my focus toward visualizing how amazing it was going to feel when I finally reached the top of the mountain.

After months of training and anticipation, the moment I had been waiting for had finally arrived. I took three centering, deep breaths and clearly envisioned myself accomplishing my goal. As I saw myself reaching the summit in my mind's eye, I instantly welled up with pride. I vividly saw my outstretched arms shoot up high above my head, raised in the universal posture for victory. I smiled excitedly to myself. I opened my eyes, eager to begin my journey up the mountain.

CHAPTER 1

The Power of Positive Thinking

Let's address the elephant in the room. For many people, the thought of becoming a millionaire feels anything but simple. As the title of this book points out, it isn't so much a destination as it is a journey. It will require commitment, self-discipline, and delayed gratification—all internal skills that can be tough to master. Luckily, you can follow a few simple principles to make your financial life much easier. The goal of this book is to demystify that process and make it both simple to understand and simple to execute. As a reminder, if you are just starting your financial journey, don't worry. This book is simple enough for someone new to the workforce to easily understand. To make it easy for everyone (at any age), we will be starting at the "beginning of the trail" as you start "the climb." Throughout this book, we will keep the concepts and wealth-building strategies simple and easy to follow. Again, if you are further down the road and not new to the workforce, you can still benefit from the information found in earlier chapters.

Far more important than your annual salary is your belief in yourself. Often, what holds people back from achieving their long-term financial goals isn't the number written on their monthly paycheck; it's the mindset they use to make daily decisions on how to spend, save, and invest their money. There is immense power in positive thinking and believing that what you are planning to do will work. If you don't have confidence in your financial plan and believe that success is possible, reaching your goals will be extraordinarily difficult.

For instance, did you know that the average person makes roughly 35,000 decisions daily? Studies have shown that 7 out of 10 people procrastinate when making big financial decisions, mainly because they lack confidence in their money management knowledge.[6] If you read this book, we promise you will not be part of the 70% of consumers who feel this way. Instead, by the time you finish reading *The Simple Road Toward Financial Freedom,* you will be equipped with the financial insight you need to do just what the title promises: pursue financial freedom.

Now, back to that elephant in the room. Let's clear something up right away. Many people might wrongly assume that we are trying to say that becoming a millionaire is easy. It's not. It's hard work. But just because something is difficult doesn't mean it has to be complicated. You may have heard the popular question, *"How do you eat an elephant?"* The answer is: *one bite at a time.* While we won't give you any culinary suggestions on exotic cuisine or comment on the ethics of eating critically endangered species in this book, we will share simple steps you can take *today* to help you achieve your goals.

Becoming a millionaire takes daily commitment. This book will show you how to pursue your financial goals. We will break it down "one bite at a time" into simple terms, simple steps, and simple equations that show you exactly how much you would need to save and by what age to potentially become a millionaire.[7] **For most people reading this book, that goal is achievable**. At first, it may take a lot of hard work, but our promise to you is that if you follow the steps laid out in this book, the road will appear to be more straightforward.

---

[6] https://www.businesswire.com/news/home/20180419005317/en/We-Make-35000-Decisions-Per-Day-but-Seven-in-10-Postpone-Major-Financial-Decisions. Author: Hillary Gebert, *We Make 35,000 Decisions Per Day, but Seven in 10 Postpone Major Financial Decisions,* 4/19/18.

[7] This example is hypothetical only, and does not represent the actual performance of any particular investments. Investments in securities do not offer a fixed rate of return. Principal, yield and/or share price will fluctuate with changes in market conditions and when sold or redeemed, you may receive more or less than originally invested.

The Millionaire Mindset

Henry Ford famously said, "Whether you think you can or you can't, either way, you're right." Many high-income earners are nowhere close to being millionaires—even though they earn hundreds of thousands of dollars per year. Debt, being house-poor, and flashy lifestyle decisions can be deceptive ways to disguise poor financial habits. According to recent stats, nearly half of those earning six figures live paycheck to paycheck.[8] On the flip side, many high-net-worth individuals earned an average income from a modest paycheck for years, saving and investing their way to wealth. The information in this book is "simple" because it applies to everyone, whether you make $50,000 per year or $500,000.

Your mindset (again, not the number written on your paycheck) is what will be the most vital to your success on the road toward financial freedom. Most people incorrectly assume you have to make a lot of money to be wealthy. The secret no one tells you is that the wealth-building principles we will share in this book don't discriminate. On paper, they will work using everyday salaries and examples that most readers can easily relate to, just as they work for rocket scientists and brain surgeons. Deciding to believe that this book can work for you is a decision that only you can make; whether you think you can or you can't is your choice.

It Won't Happen Overnight

Sure, many millionaires may look down from the top of the mountain and tell everyone else that it's "simple." But what's the *real* secret to becoming a millionaire? If you are just starting out— looking up at what appears to be a

---

[8]https://www.cnbc.com/2022/10/24/more-americans-live-paycheck-to-paycheck-as-inflation-outpaces-income.html#:~:text=Investing%20Club-,63%25%20of%20Americans%20are%20living%20paycheck%20to%20paycheck%20%E2%80%94%20incl uding%20nearly,half%20of%20six%2Dfigure%20earners&text=With%20persistent%20inflation%20erodi ng%20wage,according%20to%20a%20recent%20report. Author: Jessica Dickler, *63% of Americans Are Living Paycheck to Paycheck - Including Nearly Half of Six-Figure Earners*, 10/24/22.

mountain of money in front of you, with a peak so tall it looks like it could nearly touch the stars—the answer may surprise you.

The biggest secret to becoming a millionaire is to start thinking like one.

This may sound like a cop-out, but hear us out. Until you begin thinking like a millionaire, you won't be able to make decisions that will help you get there. Millions of people drive by Mount Shasta every day. Most look up and marvel at how tall the mountain is. Only a handful actually desire to climb up to the peak. Once they make that choice, they begin thinking like a mountain climber. But until they start thinking like a mountain climber, they don't entertain the idea of asking themselves the right questions to actually prepare themselves to go climb a mountain. Once they make up their mind to make the climb, only then do they put a plan together and start making the necessary preparations to get ready to pull it off.

The road to financial success is no different. Most of us were never taught the secrets to personal finance in school. Instead, you must accept the fact that the first step to being a millionaire is to believe in yourself and to believe that it is possible for you to make the climb. You are capable of learning what you need to do to take control of your financial destiny. Then, you must take a leap of faith to start implementing the simple steps we will share with you in the chapters ahead.

> *"If something is important to you, you will find a way. If it's not important to you, you will find an excuse."*

Someone who wants to become a millionaire knows and accepts that it won't happen overnight. Instead, they become smart and use tools like long-term growth, free money, and simple math equations to do the majority of the work for them. They accept that the actions they need to take are (for the most part) pretty simple. But what's more difficult is having the willpower and the self-control to delay gratification and take the *right action* at the *right time*.

Many people in today's world want things to happen immediately. If you press a few buttons on your smartphone, you can have a pizza at your door in twenty minutes or a package from Amazon waiting on your doorstep when you wake up the next morning. Becoming a millionaire takes time. The emotional and psychological commitment to that ideal requires consistency. The people who are most successful at staying consistent are the ones who have a crystal clear vision of their future.

Mental Mastery = Money Mastery

Mastery over your money demands mastery over your mind. One way to get in touch with your inner millionaire is to use a technique called *visualization*.

Take an opportunity to engage your imagination for a few moments so you can "look around" and imagine *how it feels to be a millionaire*. Sometimes, working to earn a living can leave you so busy that you never stop to think about what you are working toward. Stopping to intentionally pause and "look around" inside the ideal future you want to experience one day will make it easier to connect with *why you want to become a millionaire* in the first place.

Many people want to become a millionaire because they believe all their problems will magically disappear. Here's a secret—they won't. If anything, the problems you have today will only be magnified by inserting more money into the equation if that's your current viewpoint. That type of thinking is dangerously similar to the *box of chocolates approach* that keeps many people stuck. The people who use their money wisely have a plan for how they will use it and a strong reason for why they want it.

True wealth is more than just a dollar amount in your savings account; it grants you the opportunity to live your life freely. It allows you to pass on your blessings to the next generation by leaving behind a legacy. True wealth gives you profound satisfaction, not just for yourself but for your family as well. It provides a feeling of personal fulfillment. It's not just about having "made enough" money, but more importantly, true wealth is living a rich and meaningful life. What that means and how you wish to achieve it is entirely up to you. For every person, it will look a little bit different. But one thing remains the same: to achieve great wealth, you need a strong and compelling reason to put in the work to attain it.

Before you start on the road toward financial freedom, you need to get in touch with your emotional desires for wanting to achieve this goal. Not only should you think about how you will spend the money, but even more importantly, how the money can support you on your way to achieving your future goals. The average person works for 40-45 years. That's a long time to do anything. It can be a paradise, doing something you love while actively saving and investing for your financial freedom down the road. Or, it can be a living torment, slaving away at a job you hate year after year, worrying about money every time the calendar rolls into a new month.

All too often, people take the easy way out. They complain about how hard it is to follow these simple steps. They give up because they don't want to take the time to educate themselves and learn about their finances. Then, they convince themselves that these techniques and strategies are only for "rich" people and that they could *never* work for *someone like them*. Sadly, they never know what steps to take to gain control over their financial destiny. As a result, their lives are very difficult. Don't be someone who sabotages their dreams before they ever get started. Our society is riddled with limiting beliefs surrounding money that are often passed down, like hereditary traits. Wealth management isn't hereditary. Habits and lifestyle choices may be, but the good news is that how you manage your money and your mindset around financial freedom are completely up to you. For that reason, we encourage you to read this book with an open mind. Even if the advice sounds difficult or a little out of your comfort zone, we encourage you to stick with it.

One of the biggest questions you can ask yourself is, *Why do you want to be a millionaire?* Knowing *why* you want what you want helps you have an internal fire of ambition, driving you and propelling you forward. A strong and compelling *why* will make it easier to justify putting in the hours of hard work to reach the top of your mountain.

Visualization Exercise:

If you want to do this exercise and take it really seriously, then you'll need to set aside fifteen to twenty minutes to just clear your mind and follow along.

1. **Relax**

   Get into a meditative state, do some yoga, or throw on some relaxing music or white noise for ten to fifteen minutes. Light some incense or candles, turn off your cell phone, put on noise-canceling AirPods, or whatever you do to gently bring yourself into a relaxed state where you can fully tap into the power of your imagination.

2. **What Do *You* Really Want?**

   The goal of this exercise is to help you live your life by design, not by default. Everyone's individual wants will always be unique because what motivated your parents won't motivate you, and vice versa. If you don't take a look around at what you want for your future self, you could end up looking back twenty years from now, miserable. Instead, we invite you to reflect on what really matters. Before we start sharing financial principles and advice to help you on your road toward financial freedom, it's important to get clear on what you want out of life. No amount of money can buy happiness, but it can buy you the freedom to live a meaningful life.

   Reflect on the following questions. Read each question carefully and then spend a few minutes diving into the thoughts and feelings that arise for you. You don't need to have concrete answers just yet. Use these questions as a bridge to bring you into a space that allows you to go beyond the mental chatter of your mind and enter into a future where your dreams can become a reality.

Ask yourself:

-What do I really want to create in the next 40 years?

-What values do I want to embody as an individual?

-What are my unique gifts and talents?

-What specific actions do I want to take in the world that will help me to make an impact?

-Who do I want to help serve with my unique gifts and skills?

-What bigger purpose am I striving to fulfill in my life?

-What is my mission (summed up in a single sentence or two) that I believe in strongly? Would people who knew me well say the same about me?

-What types of goals motivate me to be my most authentic self?

-What types of challenges make you jump out of bed in the morning, ready to take on the world?

-What's a cause you care about that you aren't afraid to speak up about?

-What passions do you wish to develop and master over the next 40 or 50 years?

3. Visualize the Summit

Now that you've reflected on some of life's big and enduring questions, it's time to think about what you want the pinnacle of your life to look like. Likely, if your dreams are anything like the average American's, your dreams for your future will require you to manage your finances wisely and be prudent about where your money goes. This is a time to get excited about what you really want. Don't forget to think about the bigger picture and all of those "tough-to-answer" questions we just shared above—those matter a lot more on your path to creating *true wealth* than the square footage of your house or if you drive the latest series BMW.

When you were a child, before a big birthday or holiday, you probably went to sleep dreaming about the presents you would open the next day. Similarly, it's important to visualize what the top of the mountain looks like for you. What would it feel like to reach the summit of your financial mountain? For most of us, what comes to mind immediately are the material items that make up a part of our lives. There's nothing inherently wrong with that. Your occupation, income, family size, zip code, and real estate investments all play a role in your future decision-making process, so it is inherently valuable to ask yourself these questions. Finding your "peak" is vital to knowing and understanding yourself as a self-aware individual capable of making changes in your life to achieve an ideal outcome.

The point of this exercise isn't necessarily to think about being rich and famous and living like a movie star. The goal is to really zero in on *what it would take for you to be happy financially.* If you need a mega-mansion high up in the hills of Los Angeles to attain happiness, then know that about yourself. If you could get by living in a 1,000 sq. ft. two-bedroom apartment and traveling abroad on a two-week vacation every year, then know that. It doesn't matter what you choose. There's no judgment of whatever type of lifestyle you want to live. But before you commit to working for decades and saving money, it's important that you know what you really want.

-How big is your house?

-What type of neighborhood do you live in?

-Do you have a family?

-What do you do for work?

-How often do you travel?

-What type of car do you drive?

-What properties do you own?

-How does having these things make you feel?

-What's missing in your life? What are the unknowns, challenges, or mysteries that come up for you when doing this exercise?

4. Find Your Path to Your Peak

Now that you've primed your mind to start thinking about your desired future outcome, it's time to focus on scaling the summit. This exercise can be transformational if you think about your vision daily. Remember, motion controls emotion. The more you consistently exercise this part of your mind, the easier it will become to program yourself to start thinking about your ideal future. Multiple times throughout your day, ask yourself, *Is my next action getting me closer or further away from my ideal self?* Think about how emotionally rewarding it will feel to accomplish these goals.

Then, imagine a much different scenario. Visualize what it would feel like if you spent money frivolously, never really tracked your budget, and never set aside any money for retirement. Imagine how defeating that would feel, watching all of your friends travel the world and go on expensive vacations with their children while you're stuck in a job with very few prospects for financial freedom.

You must be able to maintain focus, but to do so, you need to know where you want to go. If you can set a clear visual of your goal and are able to see it, it can help you maintain focus on that goal. Change is not easy, but with a well-defined goal, it becomes easier to start climbing toward it. Use the mental images you've created during this simple exercise to fuel your motivation as you read this book.

One of the reasons this visualization exercise is so important before starting your journey is that a lot of people say they want to be "rich." But few ever define what that actually means. It is just a moving target that changes each time their friends start earning more money, or their neighbor gets another new car. What's important is to define what "rich" means to you. Does your "rich" mean you retire at 50, 60, or never? Your vision of what a "rich" lifestyle looks like could change as you age. But one fact remains true: **the sooner you start, the more likely you are to become a millionaire.**

If your limiting belief is *I want to be wealthy,* again, you have to ask yourself on a daily basis, *Is this next action I'm about to take getting me closer or further away from my vision?* Then, decide if you want to follow through with that action or change your behavior to align with your goals. Over time, you will be able to test what works for you.

In the next chapter, we'll walk you through some guiding questions to help you uncover your unique needs and how to take the first step toward financial freedom—creating a monthly budget. Remember, everyone's path to becoming a millionaire will be a little different because everyone's circumstances (income, marital status, age, etc.) will vary. But one thing remains constant: *you have to believe you can succeed first before you can get results!*

The Simple Road Recap:

In this chapter, we discussed the power of positive thinking and how critical it is for your success in becoming a millionaire. We also offer a few helpful exercises you can use to think through your financial goals.

CHAPTER 2

Creating Your Monthly Budget

The snow-capped mountains stand before you, towering over the sunlit landscape. Up ahead lies an adventure just waiting for you to find. Amidst the natural wonder are questions about which way to go, which path to take, and who to trust for answers on your ascent up the mountain. These are all valid questions and pivotal information pieces for you to gather on your quest to get to the top. But as you embark on the climb, you are limited; you don't have time to wait around, wasting time deciding which way to go. To get where you're going, you need to know exactly where you are at every step of the journey.

In the financial world, just like mountain climbing, you must know which direction you are headed. And you will need a good "compass" to help you see where your money goes each month. To extend this metaphor: Despite all the technological advancements at their disposal today, many people are still "lost in the woods," so to speak, when it comes to knowing their monthly expenditures. This is where a monthly budget can be a life-changing tool. Just like a compass, it is incredibly simple, but it is hands down the best tool for the job.

Your monthly budget doesn't need to be fancy. It can be as simple as a pen and a piece of paper or as modern as an online budgeting app on your phone (we'll suggest a few good ones). Whatever system you use, the important key is that having a budget will always tell you exactly where you are financially. Think of it as your North Star, guiding you even on the darkest nights. When you are confused about what to do next financially, your budget can guide you to help you make clearer, more strategic decisions. This tool might sound trivial, but we assure you—creating a budget is important.

Monthly budgets come in all shapes and sizes. Hopefully, you're starting your journey toward financial freedom early in life, maybe shortly after your first full-time job. But if not, have no fear; you can still follow the suggestions below.

Some of the suggestions depend on where you are in your life stage. The key to accumulating money is to have a plan, plenty of time, and practice consistency. Letting your money grow for more than 30 years is ideal. Thinking ahead 30 years from now is enough to make your head spin. And even though 30 years may feel like an eternity to some, imagine how good it will feel knowing you are on track toward a comfortable, stress-free financial future. But having a budget isn't all about saving for tomorrow; it also helps you plan for rewarding and fun things that you can do today. Budgets take away the stress and guilt of overspending so that every financial decision you make can be made confidently. That's why breaking down your monthly budget is so important. It helps give you an easy bite-size rubric for checking in on your finances and managing your money wisely. Remember that every person earning a living needs to keep a budget. Even movie stars and CEOs need to track where their money is going every month.

Because every budget is different, everyone will have a slightly different system for creating their budget. For example, Mark's grandmother used to carry cash in envelopes in her purse. Each envelope carried just enough money for a specific purpose, such as groceries, clothing, fun, etc. When one of the envelopes was empty, his grandmother knew it was time to stop spending.

It doesn't matter which approach you use to track your monthly expenses, so long as you find a system that works for you—meaning you've taken the time to make sure your budget is accurate. The exercises in this chapter may take you a few hours to compile, but **creating a budget really is the backbone of getting on the road to financial success.**

Here's how we suggest you get started.

First, you'll need to divide your money into a few key areas: after-tax income, living expenses (we will call these "needs"), fun money (we will call these "wants"), and savings (this will include an emergency fund/short, medium, and long-term savings—which we will explain more about in the next chapter).

Flipping the Script

One of the simpler budget breakdowns that financial experts suggest (that we really like for its simplicity) is the 50/30/20 plan, where 50% of your income would go to your "needs," 30% to your "wants," and 20% to your savings.

But we suggest a slight twist to this popular budgeting division.

When you read about the 50/30/20 budget plan, it may sound like you need to follow each step in order. This means allocating 50% toward your needs, such as housing, insurance, and food, then spending 30% on discretionary expenses like dining out or going on vacation, and finally, putting the remaining 20% into savings. We recommend considering a slightly different approach. Start by budgeting 50% for your essential living expenses like rent, mortgage, or car payments, and then set aside 20% for your savings. It's crucial to prioritize saving 20% of your income before spending on wants. If you have any extra money left over at the end of the month to spend on wants, that's great, but we want you to focus on savings before indulging in discretionary expenses. For some, it may be difficult to hit the 20% savings mark initially due to location costs, debt, etc. The most important part is that you start the savings process at 5%, 10%, or 15% as you work toward the 20% target.

Another reason we advocate for this approach is that discretionary spending is the area where you have flexibility in your monthly expenditures. However, we urge you to treat your 20% monthly savings as a non-negotiable rule that you adhere to consistently every month. Prioritize your future self by diligently setting aside this money.

We like to call this revised strategy the 50/20/30 plan. The 50/20/30 plan is your go-to strategy for managing your budget and maximizing your money. It's a subtle change, but it is a powerful principle that we feel is sometimes overlooked in the conversation about creating a budget.

50/20/30 BUDGET BREAKDOWN

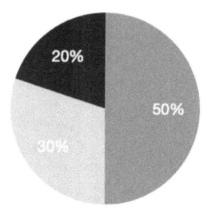

50% = NEEDS **20% = SAVINGS** 30% = WANTS

After-Tax Income

The first step in creating a budget is to calculate your after-tax income. As Benjamin Franklin famously said, "Nothing is certain except death and taxes." Almost all income is taxable, so you need to determine how much money you have coming in from various sources, such as your full-time job, any part-time jobs, and other items like child support or government benefits. Ideally, you should set up your paychecks with your employer to withhold the necessary funds for taxes, making it a planned expense rather than an unexpected one during tax season. If you haven't done this, we encourage you to speak with your employer and/or a tax advisor to learn how to set it up. Your employer can direct you to simple forms that can help calculate your withholding.

You can often get a good estimate of your after-tax income by examining your paychecks and/or your tax return from the previous year.

Is your take-home pay consistent from one paycheck to the next? Did you receive a slight tax refund last year? If you answered 'yes' to both of these questions, then you should be able to fairly easily calculate your after-tax income.

If not, for instance, if you've just started your first full-time job, there are reliable online resources where you can input your pre-tax income based on your state, and the online calculator will do the calculations for you. Be sure to consider both federal and state taxes (if applicable).

Here's a very simple example, using Pat, a fictional 25-year-old project manager:

$60,000	Salary from a full-time job in Illinois
+$2,500	Income from part-time job
$62,500	Total income

– $10,000	Federal taxes, Social Security and Medicare
– $2,500	State taxes
= $50,000	After-Tax Income

The $50,000 annually, or $4,167 per month, is the first number you will need to accurately set up your budget. This is your after-tax income. <u>Since most expenses come up monthly, we will look at our budget on a monthly basis.</u>

We also will want to remember the percentage difference between your total income and your after-tax income, otherwise known as your estimated tax rate. In this example, our estimated tax rate is 20% ($12,500 in taxes divided into $62,500 salary). <u>We will use this number later.</u>

<u>"Needs"</u>

Now, let's discuss your "needs." Items in this category include housing, food, utilities, healthcare, insurance, transportation (i.e., for commuting to your job), and any legal obligations you have to pay, such as loans or child support (essentially, where a contract has been signed). As mentioned above, additional taxes would come out of this bucket as well if not covered through your payroll deductions. The goal is to make your "needs" 50% (or less) of your after-tax income.

Here's a simple example of Pat's monthly "needs":

$1,500	Rent/mortgage
$200	Groceries
$150	Transportation
$150	Utilities
$100	Auto/Home/Renter's Insurance
$2,100	Total "needs"

<u>Savings</u>

Next, following our 50/20/30 plan, Pat needs to set aside 20% of his paycheck for his "savings." This category covers various aspects we'll discuss in more detail later, such as an emergency fund, short-term, medium-term, and long-term savings, including retirement savings. Just remember, this is the most crucial aspect of your budget because this dollar amount will grow over time to help you reach the summit of your financial goals, following *The Simple Road Toward Financial Freedom*. In our example, Pat would set aside $833 per month for savings.

"Wants"

The final bucket is for your "wants." Approximately 30% of your after-tax income should be allocated to this category. Your "wants" include dining out, hobbies, personal care, travel, entertainment, charity contributions, and more. Hopefully, you won't encounter budget constraints in the future, but if you do, this is the area you'd prioritize for cuts to ensure you can adhere to your savings plan.

Here's a simple example of Pat's monthly "wants":

$300	Going out to dinner
$300	Entertainment
$300	Travel
$200	Personal care
$100	Charity
$50	Hobbies
$1,250	Total "wants"

As you calculate your expenses, you'll want to review all the transactions that deduct money from your accounts, including your bank account (including ATM transactions), debit cards, and credit cards. While it might take some time, thinking about your monthly expenditures is not overly complicated, especially if you use online banking and can easily access your monthly statements to gauge your spending across all your accounts and cards. You just need to categorize all your expenses into either "needs" or "wants."

For the most accurate picture, we recommend examining your past expenses over the previous 12 months to understand your yearly spending average. At the very least, look at the last three months. If you have an electronic money management program like Quicken, Empower, or You Need a Budget, it will significantly simplify your budgeting process and reduce guesswork. If you aren't already using one of these services, especially the free versions, you may want to consider signing up for one of them in the future.

If your "wants" exceed 30% of your total expenses, we recommend making adjustments to align with the 50/20/30 model. This adjustment may take a few months to implement, but it's a crucial step on your path to success.

Spoiler Alert:

For a fun and eye-opening exercise, look back at the last 90 days of your credit card statements. If you could click on an item to get that money back, which item would you wish to have a do-over? The key to sticking to a budget is to not spend foolishly. Strong goals can motivate us to have the discipline to save every single month.

In summary, Pat's monthly budget looks like this:

$4,167	After-tax Income
$2,100	"Needs" (50%)
$833	Savings (20%)
$1,250	"Wants" (30%)

From here, in the coming chapters, we're going to cover how to apply your savings in the "three bucket" system.

Simple Road Recap:

In this chapter, we went in-depth on creating and analyzing your budget. This is the most important piece on your journey toward financial freedom. It is your financial "compass." We also discussed the 50/30/20 plan, or as we call it, the 50/20/30 plan, where 50% of your budget should go to "needs," 20% to savings, and 30% to "wants."

ACTION ITEM: (ideally, this should be done before reading the next chapter. Hopefully, the following template can help kick-start the process):

1. Create your personal budget.
2. Decide on savings amount.

Salary: _____

Less taxes, Social Security, Medicare, etc.   _____

After-Tax Income: _____

"Needs":   _____

Rent/mortgage   _____

Groceries/food   _____

Transportation   _____

Utilities   _____

Auto/home/renters insurance   _____

Other   _____

Savings: _____

20% of "after-tax income" above   _____

"Wants":

Going out to dinner   _____

Entertainment   _____

Travel   _____

Personal Care   _____

Charity   _____

Hobbies   _____

Other   _____

CHAPTER 3

The Three Bucket System and Risk vs. Reward

Once you've solidified your monthly budget, you should know exactly how much money is going toward your monthly expenses and how much is going into savings.

In our example, Pat is saving $833 per month.

But what do you do with all that money being set aside for monthly savings?

In this chapter, we will discuss what to do with your savings using the "three bucket" system and how it is correlated to risk vs. reward:

1. Bucket 1: "emergency" fund and short-term needs (less than two years)

2. Bucket 2: mid-term savings (2-5 years)

3. Bucket 3: long-term savings (5+ years – this includes retirement)

In summary, the investments in Bucket 1 are set up to have little risk but offer little reward. Bucket 2 investments involve more risk but come with greater potential for reward. However, with a longer time horizon, we have more time to weather a market downturn. Bucket 3 investments entail even more risk but offer the potential for even higher returns. Since our time horizon is 5+ years, we have considerable time to endure a market downturn and are more likely to witness a market uptick.

Not all savings strategies are created equal. For example, if you keep your money in a checking account, you will likely earn as little as 0% interest on your money. It sits there month after month, staying exactly the same or increasing a little if you're lucky. But while your money is sitting safely in the bank, a silent thief is reducing its value—*yearly inflation*. Inflation is constantly eroding your nest egg, which means that if you keep all your money in checking accounts throughout your life, you will effectively be *losing money*. This happens because the actual value of your money decreases over time due to inflation.

To protect against the wealth-eating nature of inflation, you can place your money into a high-yield savings account that could earn a few percent interest every year. That means that if you have $10,000 saved (assuming a 2% interest rate), you could earn $200 of "free money" just for keeping your money in a savings account vs. a checking account for one year.

But earning $200 a year won't make you a millionaire quickly. To jumpstart this process, you need to put that money into the stock market, where average annual returns are around 10% over the last 50 years. In that case, you could earn as much as $1,000 on that $10,000 after just one year.[9]

Welcome to the power of investing—one of *the strategies to getting you on your way toward financial freedom.* But each of these savings options has risks that go along with the "reward" of a higher return.

---

[9] This example is hypothetical only, and does not represent the actual performance of any particular investments. Investments in securities do not offer a fixed rate of return. Principal, yield and/or share price will fluctuate with changes in market conditions and when sold or redeemed, you may receive more or less than originally invested.

Deeper Dive on the Three Bucket System

As noted above, a simple strategy that we encourage you to adopt is known as the *Three Bucket System*. It is a simple way to approach investing and gives you an easy-to-follow framework for managing your money. The beauty of the three buckets is that they allow you to plan a strategy that safely puts your money to work in the market. Knowing that you are on the simple road to your financial goals can give you confidence.

As you accumulate and save money, that money should grow long-term if invested properly. On *The Simple Road Toward Financial Freedom*, growth will be your best friend because that yearly growth can really add up, especially if you leave your money in the market and don't touch it.

Why?

The longer your money is invested in the market, the longer it can earn *long-term growth*. If you've never looked at the numbers before, at first glance, long-term growth truly does look like the eighth wonder of the world. Watching money compound over a period of years may make it seem like there's something wrong with your calculator, but we can assure you that, while mind-boggling, the numbers don't lie.

Let's do a simple example to demonstrate the power of long-term growth. Let's go back to Pat, whose after-tax take-home pay is $50,000 per year. In our example, Pat is investing $833 per month into the stock market. Pat invests this money faithfully (and never pulls it out) in a fund that tracks the stock market, say the S&P 500. This adds up to approximately $10,000 in savings per year. If you look at his average salary, there's no way Pat would seem like a good candidate for becoming a millionaire, right? It might appear that it would take 100 years at $10,000 per year to accumulate $1 million.

Think again.

If Pat does this, starting at age 25, a little less than $250k goes into the stock market before the age of 50. Assuming an average return of 10% in his stock fund, which is slightly below the 50-year average of the S&P 500, Pat would be a millionaire in about 25 years.[10] The most important piece to pay attention to is that Pat, the new millionaire, contributed 25% of the total, and stock market returns/growth contributed 75%. When you have employers contributing to your savings, as well as an increase in your contribution due to salary growth, these numbers only get better.

With employer contributions and very reasonable salary growth, we estimate becoming a millionaire could potentially be done in about 20 years.

Our point is that even small investments like Pat's can add up to much larger numbers over long periods. Again, keep in mind that Pat's salary is likely to rise over time, meaning he will have more money to invest each month as he gets older. The more he invests, the faster he could potentially become a millionaire. These numbers demonstrate that if you leverage the power of time and let your money grow for long enough, you only need to save a portion of a million dollars to become a millionaire.

You don't have to save a million dollars to potentially become a millionaire; you just need to save and invest 20% of your paycheck every month.[11]

---

[10] This example is hypothetical only, and does not represent the actual performance of any particular investments. Investments in securities do not offer a fixed rate of return. Principal, yield and/or share price will fluctuate with changes in market conditions and when sold or redeemed, you may receive more or less than originally invested.

[11] This example is hypothetical only, and does not represent the actual performance of any particular investments. Investments in securities do not offer a fixed rate of return. Principal, yield and/or share price will fluctuate with changes in market conditions and when sold or redeemed, you may receive more or less than originally invested.

"PAT'S ROAD TO $1 MILLION"					
AGE	25	26	27	28	29
STARTING VALUE AT BEGINNING OF YEAR	$ -	$13,596	$28,959	$46,279	$65,764
STOCK MARKET RETURN @10%	$ -	$1,360	$2,896	$4,628	$6,576
401(K) CONTRIBUTION PER YEAR (@$833 PER MONTH WITH 3% ANNUAL SALARY INCREASE)	$ 9,996	$10,296	$10,605	$10,923	$11,251
COMPANY MATCH @6%	$ 3,600	$3,708	$3,819	$3,934	$4,052
TOTAL SAVED	$13,596	$28,959	$46,279	$65,764	$87,643

*ASSUMES $60,000 YEARLY SALARY WITH 3% GROWTH PER YEAR, 6% 401(K) COMPANY MATCH AND 10% STOCK MARKET RETURN

30	31	32	33	34	35	36	37	38	39
$87,643	$112,169	$139,620	$170,303	$204,557	$242,752	$285,299	$332,649	$385,299	$443,795
$8,764	$11,217	$13,962	$17,030	$20,456	$24,275	$28,530	$33,265	$38,530	$44,379
$11,588	$11,936	$12,294	$12,663	$13,043	$12,434	$13,837	$14,252	$14,679	$15,120
$4,173	$4,299	$4,428	$4,560	$4,697	$4,838	$4,983	$5,133	$5,287	$5,445
$112,169	$139,620	$170,303	$204,557	$242,752	$285,299	$332,649	$385,299	$443,795	$508,739

40	41	42	43	44	45
$508,739	$580,795	$660,692	$749,234	$847,303	$955,874
$50,874	$58,080	$66,069	$74,923	$84,730	$95,587
$15,573	$16,041	$16,522	$17,018	$17,528	$18,054
$5,609	$5,777	$5,950	$6,129	$6,313	$6,502
$580,795	$660,692	$749,234	$847,303	$955,874	$1,076,018

TOTAL SAVED	$1,076,018	
"FREE MONEY" FROM STOCK MARKET RETURNS AND COMPANY MATCH	$789,367	73%
PERSONAL CONTRIBUTION	$286,650	27%

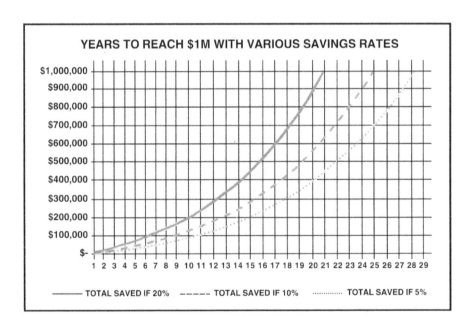

YEARS TO REACH $1M WITH VARIOUS SAVINGS RATES

——— TOTAL SAVED IF 20%   – – – – TOTAL SAVED IF 10%   ·········· TOTAL SAVED IF 5%

Risk

One very important caveat to understand before we get into the nuances of the Three Bucket System is that the stock market can fluctuate wildly from year to year. There are periods of growth (bull markets) and periods of loss (bear markets). While this seems pleasant and easy to understand, turbulent market fluctuations can make or break your financial situation if not done properly. Sometimes, the market will soar, making investors very rich. Other times, the market will plummet, leading to major layoffs, unemployment, and entire corporations going bankrupt.

The money in your portfolio will fluctuate from year to year; this is a fundamental aspect of how financial markets operate. Some years, it will be much lower than you'd prefer, while other years it will exceed your expectations. These fluctuations are normal and are part of the investment process. Just as mountain climbing requires adherence to the laws of nature, such as monitoring changes in atmospheric pressure, temperature, and oxygen levels, investing requires following the rules of the market. Unfortunately, for some people, the fear of short-term losses prevents them from taking the necessary risks to achieve their goals, which is a missed opportunity.

Remember, if you have investments that you won't be touching for 20 or 25 years, it doesn't truly matter whether the stock market goes up or down in the short term, as those gains or losses are only on paper.

For those aspiring to become millionaires, not investing is simply not an option or a risk that we believe you should take. By choosing not to invest, you are, by default, opting to allow your money to lose value due to inflation, which is in itself a poor investment.

Remember, most people *work for money*. You want your money to *work for you*!

Giving every dollar a job is an important step on the road toward financial freedom. The Three Bucket System ensures that every dollar gets put to work, balancing risk vs. reward, helping you reach your goals faster. Each bucket is directly tied to its growth potential vs. risk potential.

Simple Road Recap

In this chapter, we went in-depth on the *Three Bucket System* and how the buckets are tied to risk and returns. Bucket 1 is for your emergency fund and any needs in the next two years, and should have investments with little risk. Bucket 2 is for needs 2-5 years from now, and the investments can carry a bit more risk. Bucket 3 is for needs 5+ years from now (including retirement) and can carry investments with even more risk. However, that risk is offset by how much time we have to compensate for a potential stock market downturn and corresponding rebound.

CHAPTER 4

Opening A Brokerage Account and Bucket 1: Short-Term Savings/Emergency Fund

Before we get into the specifics of each Bucket, now is a good time to talk about where to put your savings—a Brokerage Account. Brokerage accounts are different from checking or savings accounts. A brokerage account is a special account that can only be set up at certain institutions that allow you to invest in a number of sectors, including the stock market.

We would suggest opening three brokerage accounts at Charles Schwab or Fidelity (or another similar company) to hold the money in your different buckets. Keeping them here allows you to invest in the stock market. Plus, it keeps it "out of sight, out of mind," so you aren't tempted to spend it as if it were in your checking or savings accounts.

ACTION ITEM: *Open three brokerage accounts—one account for each bucket.*

Bucket 1: Short-Term Savings/Emergency Fund

Bucket 1 is the bucket you should fill first. It is devoted to your emergency fund and short-term cash needs in the next two years (if applicable). Bucket 1 is there to give you confidence and make it easy to access your money in case you need it quickly in emergencies. It is also set up to keep your money safe so the value doesn't go down if the stock market goes down. To fill this bucket, **we suggest you have enough money to cover six months of your "needs." In our example, Pat's needs are $2,100 per month, so our goal will be to have $12,600 in Bucket 1 ($2,100 x 6 months).**

If you also have money set aside that you plan on using in the next two years, say for a down payment on a house, you would want to put those funds here. The purpose of Bucket 1 is that the funds are invested safely, so it protects your money and acts as a safety net when the unexpected happens. This fund is for emergencies like car repair, emergency room visits, or anything that is unexpected. An emergency fund will cover you in a major emergency, like losing your job.

As far as where to invest these funds, we recommend investing in something airtight, such as a high-interest savings account or a Money Market account. This will earn you some interest, but don't expect it to make you rich—that's not the point of Bucket 1 money.

Why Bucket 1 Money is so Important to Wealth Strategy

Wouldn't it be wiser to move some of that money out of Bucket 1 and into Bucket 3, where it can earn a greater return and get you to financial freedom faster? This is a great question and one that financial advisors field all the time. When the market is up, people call their financial advisor, wishing they would have allocated more money in Bucket 3 because your Bucket 1 money is earning very little interest. However, those same people are oddly silent when the market crashes. They are usually very thankful that they have two years of cash sitting in savings to keep them afloat.

Now, let's answer this question another way. You want to ensure you fill up Bucket 1 because it prevents you from pulling money out of the market prematurely from your Bucket 3 investments. For example, imagine you lose your job during an economic recession, when the stock market is down 20%, and you have all your money tied up in Bucket 3. If you have no money saved up in Bucket 1, you must pull out money from your Bucket 3 funds. Most people don't believe this is a big deal. After all, it's your money; you've saved it and likely had some nice growth.

So, what's the big deal about pulling this money out of Bucket 3? The problem is that this significantly reduces your ability to earn long-term growth. When the market corrects itself, let's say it goes up 20% the next year, you will have missed out on thousands of dollars that could have been helping you save toward retirement. When you take money out of the market, the real cost is all the missed growth. A few thousand dollars withdrawn today could potentially amount to ten times that sum decades from now.[12]

The purpose of your Bucket 1 money is to give you the confidence to *stay invested in the market* (via Bucket 3) and keep your money there, even when times are hard. That way, you are staying invested and allowing long-term growth potential to do all of the heavy lifting for you toward reaching your goals. If you constantly pull money out of Bucket 3 to pay for expenses like family vacations, a new BMW, or private school tuition, you are hurting yourself in the long run. Similarly, if you don't have your safety net money in Bucket 1, you will have to pull out money from Buckets 2 and 3 to cover emergencies. While it may only seem like a few thousand dollars today, it could be worth much more decades from now.

---

[12] This example is hypothetical only, and does not represent the actual performance of any particular investments. Investments in securities do not offer a fixed rate of return. Principal, yield and/or share price will fluctuate with changes in market conditions and when sold or redeemed, you may receive more or less than originally invested.

CHAPTER 5

Bucket 2: Mid-Term Savings

Most people reading this book should be funding Buckets 1 and Buckets 3 first. But some of you will purchase houses in the next 2-5 years or some other larger expense, where Bucket 2 will be useful. Bucket 2 is for items you may need in 2-5 years. The primary purpose behind Bucket 2 is to save up for big expenses that will be coming up in the next few years. For instance, if you are saving for a down payment on a home or car purchase, you want that money to grow faster than it would in Bucket 1, but you can take a bit more risk since your investment time frame is 2-5 years.

Remember, the longer your time horizon, the less risk you face. Since Bucket 2 is technically a hybrid account (meaning it needs to be fairly easy to liquidate but also can acquire some growth), you may want to consider investing in something that takes on a little more risk than something safe, like a CD, for example, to outpace inflation. You may want a small portion of it, say 10-25%, to be invested in sectors of the stock market that are potentially less risky (like dividend, utility, or real estate funds) vs. an overall stock market fund.

Spoiler Alert:

Not everyone will need to fund all three buckets. For some people, keeping an emergency fund and investing in long-term retirement accounts is all you will need to do, especially when you are younger. Most of Mark's clients allow more risk with their money by keeping a fully-funded emergency fund and investing the rest into Bucket 3. The only clients he regularly advises to fund all three buckets are those nearing or already in retirement. Please do not get so hung up with where to invest your money that you do nothing. The most important part is to save.

CHAPTER 6

Bucket 3: Long-Term/Retirement Savings

Bucket 3 is your long-term retirement money, where you don't need these funds for at least five years. This is the "set it and forget it" bucket. **This bucket is where you want to save the most money because it will be where you accumulate the most wealth.** For that reason, you will want to take on more risk with the funds in this bucket since history tells us the growth should be much higher, and you have a long time horizon to weather a market downturn and the corresponding market uptick. Retirement funds such as your 401(k) are the first priority to maximize in Bucket 3, especially if you have a 401(k) with an employer match.

After you land your first job out of school, having the security of a monthly paycheck can be a remarkable feeling. Packets of chicken-flavored ramen noodles, stacked as high as skyscrapers in your pantry, can now be replaced with real, edible food. Instead of living in your parent's leaky basement or a cramped, shared dorm room, you can finally afford to move into an apartment. This is an exciting high point in nearly everyone's life because it gives you your first real taste of financial independence.

It may seem overkill to even think about putting some of your monthly paychecks toward your retirement account at this stage in the game. After all, you are just getting on your feet financially, and all these new expenses seem like a much bigger priority than something that may be decades away for you.

While it's important to make sure that you cover your Bucket 1 (emergency funds) needs first, saving for your Bucket 3 retirement is one of your top priorities on *The Simple Road to Financial Freedom.* Taking time to educate yourself about the realities of retirement will help you maintain that sense of financial freedom and independence throughout your life.

Mark has a poignant example that illustrates this point. When his son was just ten or eleven years old, he spent the afternoon planting trees with his father. The tiny saplings were about as tall as pool cues, maybe 5 feet at most. Mark was excited because he knew these trees would be as tall as their family's new home one day. But his son wasn't as excited. He was very skeptical: "How could a tiny sapling grow into such a tall tree?" Mark looked down at his young son and predicted that in the next decade, these trees would be towering over their house.

Fast-forward to today, and Mark was right. The trees are now nearly thirty feet tall—six times the size they were when they were first planted. Mark had the perspective and wisdom to know the trees would flourish if given time.

The point of this story is pretty clear. Small actions taken today can lead to amazing rewards in the future. This is the wisdom and magic of the 50/20/30 rule and why it is so important to prioritize your "savings" above your "wants." We live in a society that has grown accustomed to instant gratification. **The more you can discipline yourself to delay gratification, the faster you can climb your financial mountain.**

Bucket 3 Deep Dive

Now that you've successfully created a monthly budget and learned a proven technique for managing your money, it's time to discuss one of the biggest reasons you need to save 20% of your income every month—*your retirement.* If this sounds scary, don't worry; 30% of your income can still go to things you want each month. Remember, we are saving for tomorrow with 20% and still looking at our wants with 30%.

Why do you need so much money in retirement?

When you're young, your biggest asset isn't your car or even your first home. Your biggest asset at your disposal is <u>your ability to earn a salary year after year</u>. Most of us never thought of it that way before. Saving for retirement is so important because when you retire, that asset goes away—literally overnight. Since you are no longer earning a paycheck, your monthly expenses must come from a modest Social Security check and whatever you have saved for your retirement. That means you'll need to have saved enough money to cover your monthly spending rate to sustain your quality of life.

Saving up for retirement is a lot like staring up at the top of a high mountain peak. From the ground, it looks like it's a long way away. Emotionally and psychologically, it can be hard to take money you could be spending today and put it away for a rainy day years from now. We understand that saving for retirement may not be as fun as saving up for a two-week vacation to Hawaii next year, but it is a necessary step on the road toward financial freedom. The good news is that the sooner you start saving for retirement, the easier it will be to reach your goals. But even more importantly, the earlier you begin saving, the *less money* it will take to get there. And if you stick to the 50/20/30 rule and diligently save 20% each month, reaching your retirement goals will most likely be very simple for you.

It may seem counterintuitive, but remember, time is your best friend when it comes to growing your money. The more time you allow for your money to grow in the stock market, the better off you will be. Over several decades, ideally, this investment will grow, and each time you add 20% of your monthly paycheck to your retirement accounts, you will be one step closer to reaching your retirement goals.

One of the most overlooked financial secrets is the fact that if you are in your 20s, you can save significantly less and still have more money by the time you retire than someone who is late to the game and starts investing in their 30s or 40s. The amazing part about long-term growth is that, in many cases, investing *less* money earlier can make you significantly wealthier than someone who invests *more* money later! Often, an older person would have to contribute 5 to 10 times more than someone who starts when they are young because they don't have the advantage of time on their side, which allows long-term growth in the stock market to work its magic. As we've already discussed, the benefit of long-term growth on your journey toward financial freedom seems to defy logic, but it truly is your best friend.

Now that you have a better understanding of how to use the *Three Bucket System* to manage your growing portfolio, let's take a closer look at how to strategize your Bucket 3 retirement savings.

Luckily, there are only three major retirement plans we suggest you fund: **a 401(k), an Individual Retirement Account (IRA), and a Health Savings Account (HSA),** which you can read about in the next chapter. While these three-letter acronyms may seem confusing, they are actually very simple ways to accumulate wealth for retirement. The reality is that these plans make it possible for most people to save enough money to successfully retire. Let's look at two of the most common retirement plans, 401(k) and an IRA.

401(k), 403(b), or Other Employer's Retirement Plan

For most people, one of the best retirement funds to invest in first will be your employer retirement plan. 401(k), 403(b), and SIMPLE IRA are all examples of some of the most common employer retirement plans you may be offered to participate in. Most employers will have an employer retirement plan in place that the employer sets up for you to contribute toward retirement. An employer retirement plan is so beneficial because it allows you to contribute pre-tax dollars (which saves you on the tax bill you owe the IRS every year). The other major advantage to an employer retirement plan is that most employers will "match" your investment, meaning that they will contribute a certain percentage toward your retirement plan to help incentivize their employees to begin saving for retirement. Many people overlook how incredible this opportunity to invest in your future is. **It's the equivalent of someone walking up to your desk at work and offering you thousands of dollars of free money every year.**

Using your monthly budget created in Chapter 2, you'll want to decide how much you want to contribute to your retirement accounts each month. Typically, you'll want to set up a percentage of your annual salary to go toward your employer's retirement plan. If you invest 2.5-6% of your monthly paycheck, most likely, your employer will invest an additional 2.5%-6% as well, which is essentially like getting a pay raise since the money is "free." But just because your employer may match up to 6% doesn't mean you should only invest 6% of your salary—you still want to save 20% of every single paycheck. Depending on your salary (and the threshold limits for annual contributions), your employer's retirement plan may be a great place to put that money.

Remember that every employer will have slightly different plans, so be sure to know how much they offer in employer matches before deciding how much to contribute. You should always remember that if they offer a match, *invest in this before funding other retirement accounts* because it allows you to take advantage of free money.

Let's look at how this works using some real numbers.

As mentioned earlier, Pat makes $60k per year before taxes and, let's say, contributes 5% ($3,000) of his salary to his employer's retirement plan, which is one of the most common types, a 401(k) plan. Pat prioritizes funding his

401(k) first because his employer offers a 100% full match. Based on his employer match, Pat automatically has $6,000 per year for retirement, even though he only contributed $3,000. The best part? Essentially, Pat got a $3,000 raise just for contributing to his 401(k) plan. Pat's "free money" will hopefully continue to grow year after year, and by the time he retires, that $3,000 annual contribution should potentially be worth much more.

Roth 401(k)

When you fund a 401(k) or Individual Retirement Account (which we will explain in more depth in the next section below), you save on taxes in the year you contribute. This can be great in the year when you invest in these accounts, but you will subject yourself to paying taxes on these investments when you withdraw the money, most likely during retirement. To address the issue of paying high taxes on your 401(k) earnings in retirement, many employers offer a separate type of 401(k) account that you may wish to consider called a Roth 401(k). A Roth 401(k) is a relatively newer type of retirement account that allows you to contribute <u>after-tax</u> dollars. Since you invest money that has already been taxed, you do not have to pay taxes when you withdraw your funds during retirement. (We will discuss taxes and retirement accounts further in Chapter 13 of this book.)

Quicker Path Toward Financial Freedom: Be sure to set up your company-sponsored retirement plan as a <u>percentage</u> and not a <u>dollar amount</u>. As your income increases, your savings contribution will automatically increase as well. If you set up your company-sponsored retirement plan contribution as a set dollar amount, you'd have to remember to increase your contribution, which many people forget to do.

Individual Retirement Accounts (IRA)

Another retirement plan you've likely heard of before is called an IRA, which stands for Individual Retirement Account. While 401(k), 403(b), or SIMPLE

IRA are examples of employer-sponsored retirement accounts, the IRA was designed to allow individuals to contribute toward their own retirement. Like a 401(k), there are two major types: a traditional IRA plan (known simply as an IRA) and a Roth IRA. Both are useful, and you can strategically use both to your advantage. You have to set up individual retirement accounts yourself using a brokerage account.

Let's explore some of the stipulations behind an IRA account. First, your contribution limits will be much lower than those for employer-sponsored retirement plans. For 2024, the contribution limit for a 401(k) is $23,000, while both Roth IRAs and IRA accounts have a limit of $7,000. Just like with 401(k) and Roth 401(k), you can have both types of IRA accounts. However, your total contribution limit cannot exceed $7,000 in total (for both IRA accounts).

Money that goes into an IRA account is similar to an employer-sponsored retirement account in that you get a tax break in the year you contribute (this time via your tax return), but you will pay taxes when you withdraw it in retirement (or after reaching age 59.5). With a Roth IRA, you don't get the tax break on your tax return, but you don't have to pay taxes when you withdraw it.

Aside from taxes, one major difference between a Roth IRA and a traditional IRA plan is that while most can contribute to an IRA account, you must meet certain income requirements to fund a Roth IRA. For 2024, individuals must earn no more than $161,000 to be eligible for funding a Roth IRA (or $240,000 for filing as a joint household income).

Where to Invest

Regarding where to invest your Bucket 3 funds, we recommend investing in the broad stock market through index mutual funds or ETFs, as they typically have averaged about a 10% return, have low costs and diversification, and you have a long time horizon to weather potential market downturns.

Some popular index funds try to mirror the composition and performance of the S&P 500, the NASDAQ Composite Index (generally considered tech-heavy), and the Dow Jones Industrial Average. Remember that when you invest in index funds and the market declines, you are still investing in some of the highest-performing public companies globally. It's common for people to fear losing all their money, but unless all of these companies go completely bankrupt, you won't lose all your money. You just need to be patient and trust the system. Always remember that historical averages do not predict future earnings. **In fact, if the stock market goes down, consider that your future purchases are now buying shares at a discount.**

One of the most popular indexes that funds try to emulate is called the S&P 500, consisting of the 500 largest companies in the U.S. When you invest in a fund tracking the index, you effectively purchase shares in all 500 companies simultaneously, making it a highly diversified investment. Some companies in the S&P 500 include AAPL (Apple), MSFT (Microsoft), and AMZN (Amazon).

We suggest you do your own research to find the investment that is best for you.

Simple Road Recap

In this chapter, we explained the importance of beginning your retirement savings plan early in life. We also explored why Bucket 3 money is so vital to climbing the financial mountain. We also examined the benefits of contributing to your employer's retirement plan and showed you an easy way to get "free money" through an "employer match." We explored the differences between a 401(k) and a Roth 401(k) and the differences between an IRA and a Roth IRA.

CHAPTER 7

Health Savings Account

When you are climbing a mountain, the unexpected can happen at any moment. One misstep, one wrong calculation, or an unpredicted accident is all it takes to lose your footing. Changes in elevation, weather, and even supplies and resources can cause you to have to turn back and get to base camp or risk a deadly fall. The higher you climb, the more the elements begin to wear on your body and mind. Things that didn't seem like a big deal at the start of your journey become major issues. Similarly, as you move further along on your road toward financial freedom, health issues may arise for you and your family. Unexpected medical expenses are one of the leading causes of bankruptcy, and they can account for thousands of dollars of necessary medical bills.

Your health today may not seem like a big deal, especially if your employer offers health insurance benefits. However, when you are retired, health issues can quickly become financial nightmares. The average person will spend $12,914 on unexpected health problems and medical treatments.[13] Surgeries, medications, and lengthy hospital stays when you are sick can really take a toll on the family nest egg. Worse, sometimes lengthy physical therapy or

---

[13]https://www.cms.gov/research-statistics-data-and-systems/statistics-trends-and-reports/nationalhealthexpenddata/nhe-fact-sheet. Author: Centers for Medicare & Medicaid Services, *NHE Fact Sheet*, 2022.

rehabilitation is needed to get you or a loved one back on their feet. Sometimes, in-home care or residential care facilities are needed. This type of intensive care can cost hundreds of thousands of dollars.

An HSA plan is a smart investment toward your family's financial future. It is a way to counteract some of the high costs associated with aging. And let's face it, no one has developed an FDA-approved anti-aging pill. The best we can do is to prepare and plan for the rising costs of healthcare that may be needed down the road.

The beauty behind an HSA plan is that it is a very strategic retirement account with many benefits that even the best 401(k)s and Roth IRAs lack.

However, because they are newer and not everyone will qualify for an HSA plan, they are rarely talked about. Financial advisors usually aren't incentivized to counsel clients on investing in them. Sadly, many investors miss out on the opportunity to set aside money for themselves and their families by not investing in an HSA.

HSA

The major benefit of being an HSA owner is that your contribution toward your HSA is pre-tax, meaning you never have to pay taxes on it. However, the key difference (and this is an extremely important distinction between 401(k), IRA, and HSA) is that your money can grow, and you can withdraw your money completely tax-free for qualified health care expenses. Regarding tax-saving retirement accounts, in our opinion, an HSA is one of the best tax and investment vehicles for long-term investing. **We suggest using your HSA as a long-term investing tool and not to pay near-term health care expenses. Let your "triple-tax-free" money grow.**

If your savings budget allows more than the max 401(k) match contribution, then we suggest funding a Health Savings Account.

First, let's clear up a few common misconceptions. Not everyone will qualify for an HSA account. To fund an HSA in 2024, you need to be in a qualifying High Deductible Health Plan with a minimum deductible above $1,600 for individuals or $3,200 for families and meet certain other requirements. Your maximum out-of-pocket costs must equal or exceed $8,050 for individuals and $16,100 for families.

If you qualify, you can fund your HSA up to $4,150 for individuals or $8,300 for families.

Again, if you qualify to fund an HSA, you will usually have a higher deductible for your insurance plan, which usually equates to saving money on your monthly premiums. However, having a high deductible can be costly since many health insurance plans will require you to meet your deductible before benefits like coinsurance take effect.

<u>To help compensate for the higher deductible, employers will often contribute to your account, just like a 401(k) match.</u>

Once you reach a certain threshold in your HSA account (usually around $2,000), you can invest your funds in the stock market so that you start cashing in on the potential benefits of long-term growth. An HSA account is similar to an employer-sponsored retirement plan, in which the funds aren't needed for 25+ years, so we suggest focusing heavily on stock funds.

One common point of confusion is that many people don't realize that your HSA contributions don't expire at the end of the fiscal year. An HSA is different from an FSA, or Flexible Spending Account, which used to be a popular healthcare savings plan that had to be spent before the end of the year. With an HSA, your money stays in the HSA until you use it. It also doesn't disappear if you change jobs. Rest assured, you can keep your HSA, just like you can keep your 401(k), even if you change employers or retire.

If you are someone who has a lot of medical expenses going on right now or someone where a high deductible is going to be problematic, then you may want to think twice about getting a high-deductible plan and investing in an HSA. If you do have a high deductible plan and meet the qualifications, we strongly suggest that you take advantage of all the amazing benefits an HSA offers. But don't make that switch based on purely financial reasons. Remember, this is a health care plan, first and foremost. Always make informed healthcare decisions based on your health needs and the recommendations of your primary medical care providers.

Simple Road Recap

In this chapter, we took a deep look at HSAs and why it is such a great investment tool. It's the only program that is "triple tax-free." You can use "pre-tax" money to fund the account, it grows tax-free, and you can withdraw money for qualified uses and not have to pay any taxes on your contribution OR your gain. As such, it's also a great savings tool. In addition, sometimes your employers will even contribute to your account.

ACTION ITEM: review your health plans from your employer to see if an HSA is a good option for you next year. Sometimes, you're not given a lot of time to sign up for healthcare in open enrollment, so doing your homework now may be a great option.

Author Summary Notes: Now that you have reviewed a number of critical items on your journey toward financial freedom, we thought it would be helpful to provide a quick summary of our thoughts on where to divide up your monthly savings and a few examples of what it may look like:

1a. Fund Bucket 1 (emergency fund).
1b. Fund your workplace retirement plan (401(k), Roth 401(k), etc.) up to the match amount.
1c. Fund your HSA up to the match amount.

2. Additional savings should ideally be applied to your workplace retirement plan and HSA up to the max amount unless there are needs for Bucket 2.

3. If additional savings are still possible, we suggest you fund your IRA / Roth IRA.

4. Remaining funds should be put toward non-retirement accounts in Bucket 3.

Here are a few examples for Pat ($833 per month savings), whose company 401(k) matches up to 5% of his salary of $60,000 and matches up to $500 per year in an HSA. These are just a few ideas on how to approach this. **There isn't one right or wrong answer; it all depends on your situation**.

Example 1 (no Bucket 1/emergency fund).
- $541 per month to Bucket 1 until the balance is $12,600 (six months of "needs")
- $250 per month (5% of salary) to Bucket 3 via workplace 401(k) to take full advantage of company match (where Pat will get an additional $250 per month ($3,000 per year) in "free money")
- $42 per month ($500 per year) to Bucket 3 via workplace HSA to take full advantage of company match (where Pat will get an additional ~$42 per month ($500 per year) in "free money")

Example 2 (Bucket 1/emergency fund is fully funded).
- $791 per month (15.8% of salary) to Bucket 3 via workplace 401(k). This would take full advantage of the company match (where Pat will get an additional $250 per month ($3,000 per year) in "free money").
- $42 per month ($500 per year) to Bucket 3 via workplace HSA to take full advantage of company match (where Pat will get an additional ~$42 per month ($500 per year) in "free money").

Example 3 (Bucket 1/emergency fund is fully funded and trying to save for a down payment on a house. Assuming Pat wants to put 50% toward Bucket 2 and 50% toward Bucket 3).

- $417 per month for Bucket 2 for a down payment on the house.
- $374 per month or 7.48% of salary for Bucket 3 via workplace 401(k). This would take full advantage of the company match (where Pat will get an additional $250 per month ($3,000 per year) in "free money").
- $42 per month ($500 per year) to Bucket 3 via workplace HSA to take full advantage of company match (where Pat will get an additional ~$42 per month ($500 per year) in "free money").

CHAPTER 8

Your Automatic Investment Plan

Imagine going to take the driving exam to get your driver's license. You've studied everything you need to know, and you feel confident you are finally ready to enjoy the freedom of the open road. You sit down in the driver's seat and politely wait for your driving instructor to shimmy their way into the passenger side. You're careful to first fasten your seat belt and check all three mirrors. But then you look down in horror as you see a terrifying silhouette between the two of you—*a stick shift*.

You've only learned to drive cars with an automatic transmission; how in the world will you figure out how to drive a stick in time to ace your driver's test? At that moment, all you can think about is how badly you wish the vehicle had an automatic transmission. Now, you must pay attention to every facet of the drive—speed, weather, incline, and shift gears while navigating the changing road conditions while remembering to shift gears. This may sound like the setup for a bad recurring dream, but it is actually a very poignant metaphor for your financial life.

Having an automatic investment plan gives you confidence, knowing that you are prioritizing your financial freedom every single month—even if you forget or go on vacation, every paycheck is getting you one step closer to your goal automatically. In this chapter, we will share some of the benefits of easy-to-use systems that will help you make sure you never forget to save and invest on your road to get where you're going—*The Simple Road Toward Financial Freedom.*

The Employee Benefit Research Institute asked more than 1,000 retirees between the ages of 55 and 80 their biggest regret about retirement.[14] Over half of those who completed the Retirement Reflections Survey said they wished they had started saving sooner for retirement. Despite most of the respondents being middle to upper-income Americans, half of them responded that they wish they could go back and change their financial habits to save more or start saving earlier. In other words, you need to save for retirement, and it's a lot easier if you do it early versus having to play catch up. Life has tradeoff decisions where you either go through the *"pain of discipline"* or the *"pain of not having enough."*

As evidenced by the retiree's responses above, one of the hardest aspects of becoming a millionaire is having the discipline to faithfully set aside money each month toward funding your three buckets. Recall in Chapter 1 how we asked you to visualize your future. When most people think about saving money, it's much more fun to envision a new car, new clothes, or a weekend getaway than it is to think about setting aside an extra $500 a month. Considering that retirement may be as far as 40 years away for you, it's totally understandable to feel this way. But remember how good it felt to think about having more than enough money to finance your lifestyle during the Visualization Exercise in Chapter 1? That freedom doesn't come from going into debt to buy the latest Tesla model fresh off the assembly line. Instead, that type of inner freedom comes from saving diligently and prioritizing your needs wisely first and then rewarding yourself and your family with a few toys.

---

[14] https://www.ebri.org/content/retiree-reflections. Author: Bridget Bearden, *Retiree Reflections*, 6/16/22.

We have a helpful strategy that will make sure that you never forget to prioritize your savings, and it will take the sting out of feeling like you have to sacrifice between going out to eat and saving money. It's called the *Automatic Investment Plan*. This approach is an easy way to accumulate wealth when you combine it with the other strategies in this book. The best part? It's very simple to execute, and you can do it in as little as fifteen minutes. It's one of those scenarios in life where you can do it once and enjoy the benefits for years to come.

To create an Automatic Investment Plan, you need to set up an automatic transfer each month to have money automatically move from your checking or savings account into your brokerage account. Remember, this is "out of sight, out of mind" money. If you do this early in your career with a good budget, it will become a habit, and you will never get used to having this money sitting in your checking or savings account, so you shouldn't miss it. However, if this is new for you, it may take a few months to get used to seeing less money in your bank accounts. However, it is always easier to save money *before* you have the chance to spend it. Even the best-intentioned saver can find ways to justify unnecessary spending.

To set up your Automatic Investment Plan, you will need to work with your brokerage company. That usually involves going online or making a phone call or two to authorize the transfers you want to be made. What will be important for you to decide is when you want to have the money "pulled out" from your main checking or savings account, how much you want to transfer each month, and how you want that money invested.

We suggest you set up an automatic transfer the day after you get paid. For example, if you get paid on the 15th of the month, you will want to set up an automatic transfer on the 16th. That way, you'll never really see the money in your checking account. The key to the success of your Automatic Investment Plan is consistency. Each month (or paycheck) you put away money, the more your investments should grow and the closer you will get to becoming a millionaire. Remember, even small amounts of money over time can potentially grow to large sums, thanks to potential growth in the stock market.

Let's go a bit deeper into this concept by using an example from the last chapter:

Example 1 (no Bucket 1/emergency fund).
- $541 per month to Bucket 1 until the balance is $12,600 (six months of "needs").
- $250 per month (5% of salary) to Bucket 3 via workplace 401(k) to take full advantage of company match (where Pat will get an additional $250 per month ($3,000 per year) in "free money").
- $42 per month ($500 per year) to Bucket 3 via workplace HSA to take full advantage of company match (where Pat will get an additional ~$42 per month ($500 per year) in "free money").

As you can see in this example, we need to start accumulating funds in Bucket 1. For this example, we will assume payday is the 15th and 30th of the month.

You would reach out to your brokerage and set up an automatic transfer from your checking/savings account of $270.50 on, say, the 16th of the month and another $270.50 on the 31st (or 1st of the following month). These two transfers would equal the $541 we're putting toward Bucket 1.

The next step would be to get those funds invested. So, you'd work with your brokerage to invest these funds a few days after your transfer. Let's assume your Bucket 1 money is being invested in the Money Market Fund. In this example, you would work with your brokerage to have them purchase $270.50 worth of the fund on, say, the 18th and 2nd of the month.

As you can see with this example, all of your monthly investments would be automated since the funding of the 401(k) and HSA through work would be automated as well.

Also worth noting is that these transfers can always be adjusted or canceled. If your budget changes and you need to cut the transfer amount, you can always do so (provided you give enough notice).

Review Your Budget Regularly

You may be thinking that the Automatic Investment Plan sounds pretty simple. That's great! But just because it's simple and automatic doesn't mean you don't have to do anything.

It's also important that you revisit your monthly budget and yearly portfolio numbers regularly a few times a year. You'll want to revisit this to make sure that your savings goals are commensurate with your yearly salary and that your overall portfolio is headed in the right direction. If you get a $10,000 raise and don't review your automatic investment plan, you are much more likely to spend that money instead of investing it. Remember to check in on your automatic investment plan regularly and adjust it quarterly to ensure you don't miss anything. While some people will do this like clockwork, unfortunately, most will not. This leads to more money being left in their checking or savings account, which typically leads to extra money being spent. As Bill Gates warns, "Automation applied to an inefficient operation will magnify the inefficiency."

Simple Road Recap:

In this chapter, we discovered a simple strategy that will help you save every month automatically. By working with your brokerage, you can set up automatic withdrawals that automatically remove money from your checking account into your brokerage accounts, where they can immediately be invested.

ACTION ITEM:

Reach out to your brokerage and set up an Automatic Investment Plan. $_____ per (paycheck, month, etc.) on this date: _____. Once in account, invest in XXX.

CHAPTER 9

Investing Overview

"The best time to plant a tree was 20 years ago.
The second-best time is now."

- Chinese proverb

Brokerage company Charles Schwab conducted a study[15] to see if savvy investors could "time the market." Many people new to the world of investing are looking for the right time to buy and sell to maximize their profits and minimize their losses. While there's nothing wrong with wanting to earn more on your money, trying to time the market perfectly can be a difficult task, often with a low success rate. But don't just take our word for it; let's look at Charles Schwab's study to see what they found.

For this experiment, they used the baseline of a 20-year investment of $2,000 per year invested into the S&P 500 index. They took five of the most common investment mindsets and hyperbolized them into five distinct caricatures of investors. "Peter Perfect," "Ashley Action," "Matthew Monthly," "Rosie Rotten," and "Larry Linger." (Obviously, these are not based on real people, but the numbers they extrapolated are very real.)

---

[15] https://www.schwab.com/learn/story/does-market-timing-work. Author: Schwab Center for Financial Research, *Does Market Timing Work?* 9/13/23.

Peter Perfect

Peter was bound and determined to time the market perfectly. Every day, he would analyze in-depth critiques of the market. His vast knowledge allowed him to invest $2,000 into the market every single year when the stock market was at its lowest point. (Meaning, he bought the stocks at their lowest value each year for twenty straight years, something that is basically impossible.)

Ashley Action

Ashley didn't have time to study and read up on the market trends like Peter. Instead, she invested the money the minute she got it. That way, she wasn't tempted to spend it. Every year, she repeated this simple habit for twenty years. She completely took the guesswork out of the equation and kept it simple.

Matthew Monthly

Matthew decided he would try a monthly investment approach. Each month, he invested one-twelfth of his $2,000 into the market. This made it manageable for him to stay on top of investing while also managing his monthly expenses. For Matthew, this was an incredibly simple solution that didn't require much planning—it was automatic.

Rosie Rotten

Rosie received some bad financial guidance from friends and family. Every year for 20 years, she tried to time the market and bought into it at the highest point. (Meaning, she paid the highest dollar amount per share for that calendar year, for twenty consecutive years, again, something that is basically impossible.) Whether it was a lack of financial literacy or just "rotten" luck, Rosie was very far from anything like "Peter Perfect," but she was diligent about investing every year.

Larry Linger

Larry was a bit paranoid about having all of his money tied up in the stock market. Each year, he felt a major crash was coming, so he waited to invest all of his money when the share prices were at an all-time low. One day, this would happen. Larry's lingering doubt left him devoid of any type of financial strategy, so he just left his money in cash because the perfect time to buy never came.

The Results?

After 20 years of investing $2,000 per year ($40,000 total), these are the 20-year results:[16]

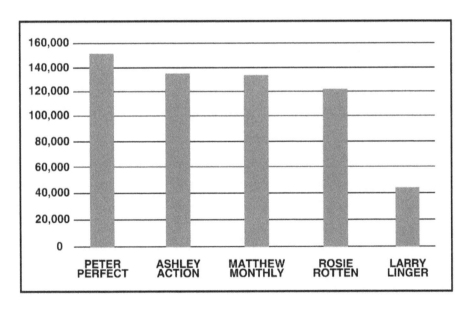

---

[16] This example is hypothetical only, and does not represent the actual performance of any particular investments. Investments in securities do not offer a fixed rate of return. Principal, yield and/or share price will fluctuate with changes in market conditions and when sold or redeemed, you may receive more or less than originally invested.

The Conclusion of this Experiment

Bad timing trumps inertia, so don't wait to start investing.

The difference was that "Peter Perfect," who found the perfect days to invest in the market every year for 20 consecutive years, only performed better than "Ashley Action's" invest immediately strategy by $15,920. That is not a huge difference in the grand scheme of things, especially when compared with "Larry Linger," whose money earned him just $44,438 in 20 years by leaving it in cash. Even if you have "rotten luck" like "Rotten Rosie," you can still potentially earn three times more by investing in the stock market over leaving your money sitting in cash.

But let's back up a minute and start with a simple question: *Why do you need to invest your money?*

There are many pathways to becoming a millionaire by wisely investing your money. You've probably seen a few pundits discussing investing on YouTube, TikTok, and cable news. Wherever you tune in, you will find dozens of talking heads offering different investment strategies that promise to make you wealthy. From cryptocurrency to day trading, it seems like everyone has a get-rich-quick strategy to sell these days. For this book, we've stuck to only the most trusted approaches to eliminate unnecessary risk and make it as easy as possible for you to get started investing.

In Chapter 3, we discussed the problem of inflation and the reasons why it's not a good idea to leave all your money sitting in a checking account. To combat inflation and accelerate your journey toward financial freedom, we suggest investing your money in the stock market to earn a return. Remember, the advantage of doing so is that your money will potentially grow over the long term. Year after year, this growth will snowball into a much larger sum, meaning you can potentially become a millionaire while only saving a small percentage of a million dollars. If that sounds much better than trying to save up a million bucks, keep reading.

Let's use a metaphor for thinking about the importance of investing your money—*the seed*. Every pound of produce you buy at the supermarket, from crisp green heads of lettuce to ripe nectarines or flavor-bursting Bing cherries, starts out as a tiny seed. The seeds are very cheap to procure, costing just a few pennies. Nature's miraculous power to grow and expand is inside each of these seeds. Seeds cost only a few cents, whereas buying fully grown, mature fresh fruits and vegetables at the store can cost 10 to 20 times more than the seeds. So, why don't we all just grow our own fruits and vegetables? (After all, we would save a tremendous amount of money over the course of our lives if we did.) The answer is *time*.

Growing your own tomatoes and kale for salads or berries for fruit smoothies takes a lot of time, energy, and money to plant and harvest. While it is much cheaper to buy the seeds today than it is to buy a carton of blueberries at the store, the big difference is that you can't eat a seed today. Instead, you have to wait for it to grow. For the sake of convenience, most of us just go to the grocery store instead of tending to our home gardens. We aren't paying for the cost of the seed; we are paying for the convenience of being able to eat the fruit or vegetable today.

Investing in the stock market is a necessary step on the pathway toward financial freedom. Investing is very similar to buying and planting seeds. (It's no coincidence that "seed capital" is an investment term referring to early-stage investors in a company.) The millionaire is focused on growth over time rather than having their money today. Instead of saving up to buy a warehouse full of produce one day, the millionaire invests their money in planting seeds today that, if appropriately cared for over time, will multiply. After all, the genetic design of a seed is to grow and expand into something much larger. Investing follows this same sort of natural order. You can invest just a fraction of your annual salary and, over time, potentially walk away a millionaire. The key is to allow enough time for long-term growth to germinate and work its magic. For this growth-generating magic to work, you also have to have the discipline to leave the seeds alone and let nature run its course.

One of the most discouraging aspects of investing for new investors is that sometimes, their investments will lose value due to fluctuations in the market. This feels foreign to many investors. After all, we are accustomed to the price of something being the price—end of story. However, we would challenge that assumption.

Week after week, the prices of items at your local grocery store are constantly going up and down. But you probably don't stop to panic because the cost of a gallon of milk went up $0.30. Likewise, you probably don't rush out and buy multiple refrigerators to start stocking up on gallons of 2% when the price of milk goes down $0.25. As ridiculous and unlikely as this analogy may seem, it is the very mindset that many investors embody. Imagine a farmer spending an entire afternoon planting seeds only to dig them back up two weeks later to sell them for double their value because the price of watermelon seeds went up $0.02 apiece. It makes no sense because the real ROI (Return on Investment) isn't from the price of the seed. The real ROI comes when you commit to the plan and allow time to do its job.

But for the average person, understanding how the stock market works seems mysterious. (We're pretty positive no one has ever tried to explain it to you using a seed analogy.) Instead, you've likely seen the tiny acronyms flash across the bottom of the screen on the nightly news or seen the Stocks app on your phone in what looks like a bizarre foreign language. If you've ever been confused by what all those percentages and letters mean, don't worry. Here's a very simplified explanation of how it all works. To make it easy to understand, we are going to give you the Cliff Notes explanation. Keep in mind that there is a lot of nuance to the global financial markets, and we could write an entire book about strategies and methods for investing.

Let's get a little technical for a moment. You've probably heard of the term "securities trading" before. A security is a financial instrument that holds monetary value. Equity securities are traded on the stock market, while debt securities are used for things like CDs and bonds that have to be held for a certain period before you receive the money you are owed. But by far, the most common form of securities trading involves buying stock in companies, which is what you are probably most familiar with and what most people think of when they hear the term "investing."

We've already shared that the long-term performance of the stock market has been about a 10% annual return over the last half-century. However, that's just an average. In some years, the market will surge far beyond that, and in other years, it might plummet. This fluctuation is natural. But because of these constant changes, picking individual stocks can be very challenging, even for the sharpest minds on Wall Street.

Knowing how an individual company will perform in the long run is somewhat unpredictable. This is why many people wrongly assume that the stock market is like gambling. The investing world is filled with stories of people who "lost it all" due to the downfall of companies when their predictions were off the mark. Conversely, others, like the earlier example of Forrest Gump's character who invested in a "fruit company" called Apple Computers, cash in big when they make the right call.

A Simplified Approach to Investing

The basic concept behind mutual funds and ETF index funds is that they allow you to pool your money with other investors to invest in multiple companies simultaneously. The "fund" is filled with various companies—usually grouped by size or geography. Investment fund managers are selected by Mutual Fund companies who choose stocks within certain criteria, usually stocks that will potentially earn their investors a good return. In exchange for (hopefully) selecting the securities in the fund, the fund company charges fees that are disclosed in the fund's investment prospectus. But be careful: even though that number sounds innocently small, over forty years, it can account for thousands of dollars lost to commissions.

An index fund, on the other hand, is a preselected list of companies. An investment fund manager doesn't choose the stocks in the index funds, so the fees you pay will be much lower.

We suggest you focus on index funds with your investments, specifically an S&P 500 Index Fund.

Investing Myths

As a financial advisor, Mark often hears clients discuss financial myths about investing. Thanks to sources like social media, many of these have become mythologized in our current society. Let's debunk a few common myths that he hears every month.

Myth #1: *Investing in the stock market is like gambling.*

Reality: With investing, the goal is to make a profit. With gambling, somebody wins, and someone ultimately loses. When you invest in an S&P 500 Index Fund, the chances of losing all of your money—because all 500 companies in the fund (Microsoft, Apple, Amazon, etc.) go bankrupt—are virtually impossible.

Myth #2: *You can time the stock market.*

Reality: As we highlighted earlier in this chapter, timing the stock market is very difficult because you have to make two correct decisions—when to buy and when to sell. We think the best plan is to invest your money when you have it - don't wait.

Myth 3: *If I am at a loss of 20%, I only have to go up 20% to break even.*

Reality: If you started with $100,000 and are down 20%, you are at $80,000. To get back to even, you will need to increase the $80,000 by 25% to return to $100,000. You have less money to work with; thus, a higher percentage is needed to reach your breakeven point.

Myth #4: *I own several mutual funds, so I am diversified.*

Reality: There is potential for overlapping stock holdings in each mutual fund or ETF, meaning it's likely less diversified than you think. If you are heavily invested in Technology funds, like many investors, you are less diversified than you may imagine, as virtually all funds will hold the large brands like Apple, Google, Microsoft, etc.

Simple Road Recap

This chapter explored the importance of investing in the stock market. We explained the seed analogy for investment growth and examined how stocks work. We also discussed the average returns expected by the stock market and some of the easiest forms of investing, such as index funds and mutual funds. Lastly, we debunked some of the most common investment myths.

CHAPTER 10

Building Credit and Your Credit Score

As you prepare to climb further up the mountain, you may think you are ready, but have you actually tested your physical aptitude? A fitness test is one easy technique to see how prepared you are for your climb. Have you spent your mornings climbing stadium stairs with a weighted vest on to test your body under pressure? Have you put in the extra effort to run hills in your neighborhood to get used to the feeling of lack of oxygen so your lungs aren't shocked during the climb? If you are serious about a successful climb, a fitness test is important to ensure you are ready. But your financial life is no different. In this chapter, we will explain a type of *financial fitness test* that every person (like it or not) must take.

Your financial future revolves around one very important number that will be attached to almost every aspect of your financial identity—your credit score. Luckily, this number is within your power to control. A credit score is a snapshot of your "creditworthiness" that banks and financial institutions use to decide whether to offer you credit. It measures how you have handled your debts and financial obligations in the past. Just like your physical fitness is a lagging indicator of how well you have trained your body, your credit score is a lagging indicator of how well you have managed your finances. Little things (missed payments or canceled credit cards—which we will explore later in this chapter) can have serious repercussions on your credit score, proving to lenders that you may not be ready for the next stage of the climb.

Credit is not the same as your earned income in your monthly paycheck. Credit is borrowed money you must eventually repay (usually with interest). There are two basic players in the financial world: borrowers and lenders (also called creditors). Homeowners, renters, and individuals are considered borrowers because they are using lenders' money when they apply for a loan, a mortgage, finance a car, or open a credit card. Lenders are the banks, private moneylenders, and financial institutions providing money in the form of credit that must be repaid over time.

Your credit score is incredibly valuable to your financial health because it will be the first thing that a landlord, car dealer, or bank checks before allowing you to rent, lease a vehicle, or receive a loan. Every time you fill out an application to rent an apartment, get a new job, open a new credit card, finance a car, or switch auto insurance companies, your credit score comes into play.

Think of it as having a significant number written on your forehead with a permanent marker, visible to every employer, landlord, and bank as soon as you walk in the door.

A high score can lead to lower interest payments, while a poor score will cost you in the form of more expensive payments with high interest, or it could even result in outright denial of your application.

Since money management is a good gauge of human behavior, the better you manage your credit, the more dependable you will appear to banks on paper as a borrower. While something as minor and insignificant as missing a payment on a credit card may not seem like a big deal, it can lower your credit score. Simple mistakes like this one will be visible on your credit report for years into the future.

Understanding Credit Scores

The concept of a credit score is fairly simple to understand once you know all the factors at play. However, many of the rules used to calculate a credit score often defy logic and common sense. For instance, you might think it is a good idea to cancel a credit card you no longer use, but in reality, this may lower your score. That's why it's important to know exactly how that score is calculated and what the various elements that go into a credit score can mean for your financial future.

A credit score is calculated based on several factors that credit reporting agencies use to determine your score. These independent agencies collect information and data about your financial history and provide it to banks. They use this information to create what is called a credit report—a file that shows banks everything they need to know about your debts, payment history, credit applications, income, and even legal factors such as tax liens.

There are three credit reporting agencies: Equifax, Experian, and TransUnion. Each bureau uses slightly different algorithms and models to calculate your credit score based on the information they have on file about you. Depending on which bureau creates your credit report, your score may differ from one agency to another—for example, your score on your Equifax credit report might differ from that on TransUnion or Experian. This variation occurs because each bureau produces its own credit report. Often, the scores are very similar. However, if there is a large discrepancy, it's usually a red flag that you need to file a dispute due to an inaccuracy on your report.

Typical credit scores range from 300-850. An example of good credit score ranges are below:

670-739 GOOD

740-799 VERY GOOD

800-850 EXCELLENT

Despite the fact that credit score ranges start at 300, a healthy credit score is in the 700 range. An excellent credit score is anything over 800. Anything in the 600 range or lower is suspicious to lenders and usually means that your application may be rejected or you will only be approved for loans with high-interest rates. However, when you are just starting out, you will need to build your credit over time before you can reach the 700-800 range. This is why it is absolutely critical to start building credit when you are young. If you are just starting out, ask your parents to add you as an "authorized user" to help build your credit score. If your parents have a high score, it will assist you in building your score more quickly. Just remember, it takes time, persistence, and a good understanding of how credit scores work to raise your score. But what do these mysterious numbers actually mean? And how are they calculated?

How Your Credit Score is Calculated

Your FICO credit score is calculated based on several factors, and each factor has a different amount of influence on your overall score.

35% Missed Payments

More than a third of your overall score is determined by how many missed payments you have. Missed payments are a major red flag and will quickly hurt your credit. We suggest putting all credit card payments on autopay to pay off the full balance each month. Even if you can only pay the minimum amount for that month, it's important to pay it on time every month. Otherwise, it can drastically lower your credit score.

30% Revolving Utilization

Nearly a third of your credit score is calculated based on how much of your total credit card limit you "utilize." Credit reporting agencies like to see that you aren't using a high percentage of your total credit limit because it shows that you won't be getting into debt. Using no more than 25% of your credit limit in a given month is recommended. For example, if you have a $10,000 credit card limit, you should charge up to $2,500 on that card per month. Your credit score might drop if you utilize more than 30% of your credit limit. Since utilization makes up 30% of your total score, it will significantly lower your credit score. Remember, just because you have available credit doesn't mean you should use it. Credit is not the same as cash.

10% Inquiries

Almost every time you fill out an application for a credit card, a new insurance policy, an apartment, or a loan it is considered a credit "inquiry" because you are inquiring about receiving new credit, hoping to be approved. There are two types of credit inquiries. The first is known as a "soft pull," which occurs when an auto insurance company checks your credit score. Credit reporting agencies allow institutions to look up your credit report (for a fee), and it doesn't impact your score.

The second type of credit inquiry is known as a "hard pull." Any time you apply to open up a credit card, bank, auto loan, etc., this is known as a hard inquiry and will usually temporarily lower your score by about 10-15 points. Each hard inquiry will stay on your credit report for months or even years. You will want to be strategic when you apply for credit cards and loans because multiple hard inquiries within a six-month period can make you appear desperate for credit and can significantly lower your credit score.

15% Length of Credit History

Your length of credit history can account for up to 15% of your score. The longer you've had open credit lines, the easier it is to increase your score. When you start out, you will start with 0 months of credit history, so your score will probably be low. To raise your score (for your first car purchase or to rent a nice apartment), you will need to have open lines of credit and prove you can be a financially stable borrower over time (usually multiple years). This is why it is absolutely critical to start building your credit score as early as possible when you are young.

10% Total Number of Accounts

Creditors like to see a diverse mix of credit types. For example, if you have multiple credit cards, a mortgage, and an auto loan, you will be seen as more trustworthy than if you only have a single card. It is important to have multiple accounts of different types open for as long as possible to help improve your credit score.

Credit scores are fairly simple to understand once you know all the basics. However, there are a few advanced points that warrant deeper discussion and more detail. Knowing these tips can help you get a better credit score, increasing your chances of getting credit when you need it and lowering the interest rates you'll pay. The less money you owe and the less debt you have, the faster you could potentially become a millionaire.

Credit Tips

- To prevent identity theft, we suggest you "freeze" your credit report and only unlock it for short periods of time, such as 24-48 hours when you need to apply for credit.
- Check your credit report yearly to find any disputes or discrepancies. Sometimes, the information the credit reporting agencies hold on file is incorrect and can damage your credit score without you even being aware of it.
- You can order your credit report to determine if any details are inaccurate. Go to AnnualCreditReport.com to see your reports for free.
- If you don't have any credit yet, you may want to become an authorized user on a credit card or apply for a secured credit card.
- Explore sites like RentalKharma.com to report rent and utility payments to credit agencies to help raise your score. Experian Boost also claims to help to boost your credit score. There may be activation and monthly fees charged for using this service, so do your research.

Simple Road Recap:

In this chapter, we looked at the importance of your credit score (and credit report) in helping you climb the financial mountain faster. We also discussed credit cards and how they can be useful tools in your financial journey. Because credit cards come with high-interest rates, we also provided some tips for responsible credit utilization.

CHAPTER 11

Don't Throw Away Free Money

On the climb up the mountain, many people overlook the little things in their backpacks that add weight. The heavier their packs, the harder the climb. The same is true with climbing the financial mountain on your way toward financial freedom. The more you spend, the slower you'll climb. The more you save, the faster you'll climb.

We've already discussed the importance of "free money" in terms of maximizing your 401(k) employer match and HSA contribution, but there are dozens of other areas of your life that likely have "free money" just waiting for you to take. Often, people get hung up on the difficult actions that can make them millionaires—like getting a higher-paying job. In reality, simple actions like watching the little things that can really add up are also very important. This is an important millionaire mindset to adopt.

Aristotle said, "We are what we repeatedly do. Excellence, then, is not an act but a habit." Getting into the habit of looking for free money is an important millionaire mindset. Now, we're not talking about picking up change on the ground every time you see pennies in the parking lot, but training your habits to not overlook these areas of financial savings is important.

One area that is extremely important is the percentage of your income you are saving. As a general rule (going back to Chapter 2), we suggest saving 20% of your income. That's just a starting point. Your pathway toward financial freedom will become much easier if you save more than 20% of your income. If you are having trouble saving 20% of your income, or you'd like to jumpstart your progress to reaching a million dollars in your portfolio sooner, we suggest you apply these "free money" principles toward your savings goals.

When you begin adopting money-saving habits, it will leave you with more money in your checking account each month. While it can be tempting to spend this extra money, we encourage you to save it instead. A quote of sage wisdom from one of our Founding Fathers, Benjamin Franklin, is, "A penny saved is a penny earned." While the math doesn't quite check out on its own, the sentiment behind it is pretty clear. If you save your money, it's yours to keep; if you spend your money, it's no longer yours.

If you apply Ben's famous phrase to the power of investing, he might be onto something. Saving an extra $20 a week may not seem like a big deal, but compounded over time, the numbers are pretty extraordinary. Similarly, saving an additional 2% more of your annual salary per year could shave years off your retirement age. The numbers may seem small, but even small numbers are important when you add them up over time. After mentoring thousands of clients and hundreds of employees, we've come up with a few ideas over the years. Even if you incorporate just one of these ideas, it should help cover the cost of this book by 2 to 3 times!

Credit Card Rewards Programs

Credit cards are among the most heavily marketed products on the planet. And for good reason: they can be incredibly helpful tools with some of the best rewards programs available to consumers. However, not paying your balance at the end of the month can be one of the costliest financial mistakes you'll ever make in your life. With an average APR just north of 20%, credit cards are expensive.

A word of caution about credit card debt: At the top of your monthly credit card statement, you'll see a little box that shows you just how long it would take to pay off your balance if you only make the minimum payment each month. Often, depending on the exact balance amount, this number could span years before it's paid off, with interest rates that could be higher than the original amount you charged. They have the power to offer you some of the best free perks on the planet or lock you into paying off extremely high interest.

<u>For that reason, it's important to use credit cards only if you're financially responsible enough to pay your balance in full every month.</u>

Many credit cards offer 1% to 2% cash back as a perk for using the card for all types of purchases, while some select cards offer up to 3% cash back for specific categories such as groceries or gas. If you pay your balance in full at the end of each month, it's equivalent to the credit card company discounting your purchases by that percentage each month. Now, 2%-3% may not sound like much, but it adds up quickly. For instance, assume you pay for your food and all your needs and wants using your credit card instead of a debit card. Using our monthly budget example from Chapter 2, these expenses would total $3,350 a month on your credit card bill. If the credit card company offers 2% back, it's the equivalent of them giving you a $67 discount on your purchases per month. Over the course of a year, that number adds up to $804. That's almost $1,000 a year in "free money." You're going to make those purchases anyway, likely using a plastic debit card, so this one simple action allows you to save more than $800 a year.

Now, some credit card loyalty programs offer free hotel rooms or airline flights instead of cash back. These can also really add up. Considering that the average hotel room is around $145 a night and the average cost of a domestic flight is north of $200, these savings can be substantial. Always do the math on the percentage you get back. Sometimes, a cash-back credit card at 2%

might be better than a hotel or airline credit card. There are websites available to consumers that can help you determine the "value" per dollar spent.

Loyalty Programs

With little to lose, it's always a good idea to join loyalty programs from places you visit more than once. Typically, these programs are free to join. Just make sure you're smarter than the marketer: don't let the reward programs drive your behavior. This means if you eat out twice per week, don't start eating out three to four times per week just because you're part of a loyalty program. Loyalty programs are a great way to save money on items you would already be purchasing.

Your "Restaurant Habit"

Eating is an essential part of the human experience. It's also expensive unless, of course, you are among the 1% of the population harvesting your own food from seeds you've planted. Going out to eat is a nice luxury but can significantly increase your spending. Even with rising grocery prices and inflation, dining out is still costlier than eating at home. If you regularly eat lunch at local restaurants five times per week during workdays, consider brown-bagging your lunch just twice a week. You'll likely save close to $100 per month.

Let's use a relatively wallet-friendly restaurant like Chipotle as an example. Imagine you make the pilgrimage to your local land of burrito goodness at least once a week. The cost of a chain-friendly burrito, chips and salsa, and a soda at a place like Chipotle is around $12 plus tax (and optional tip). Let's round up to $15 to account for those costs.

At the grocery store, you can often buy two pre-made frozen burritos, a bag of tortilla chips, a two-liter of Coca-Cola, and a non-name-brand jar of salsa for $15, which would give you at least two meals. If you ate Chipotle four times a month, that would cost around $60, whereas substituting that with grocery store burritos would cost $30 a month or $360 a year. Now, we're not suggesting you never eat at Chipotle again, but making food at home could help you invest more of your hard-earned money.

Here's another example: consider making your own tacos or hamburgers at home. Purchasing ground meat, taco shells or buns, and the necessary fixings (like lettuce, tomatoes, and cheese) would allow you to prepare several meals at home. Depending on where you shop, you could make a batch of tacos or hamburgers for a family for around $10-$15. This homemade approach offers savings and gives you control over the ingredients, allowing for healthier options. If you typically eat out, making this switch even just a few times a month could save you a significant amount of money in the long run, money that could be saved or invested for future growth.

Costco, Sam's Club, Aldi or Trader Joe's

Speaking of grocery stores, one of the best ways to save money is to shop smarter. Stores like Costco and Sam's Club offer great quality products at unbeatable prices if you are willing to buy in bulk. By purchasing more of the items you are likely to use anyway, these membership stores pass the wholesale savings on to you. Keep in mind, though, that just because the prices are lower on average, you are getting more quantity for your money. Despite the plethora of free samples throughout the store, Sam's Club and Costco aren't great places to try "new" foods that you're unsure about liking. This isn't a paid endorsement; it's simple math. The more you buy at once, the cheaper the price per ounce or unit of whatever food you purchase.

Stores like Aldi and Trader Joe's offer great products at great prices.

Try this trick the next time you go to the supermarket: At the bottom of the price sticker below any item on the shelf, there is a small number indicating the "price per ounce" or "price per unit.' This is a quick way to compare the actual costs of multiple brands to see which one truly gives you the best bang for your buck. Package size, advertising, and different measurements (oz. vs. lb.) are clever ways companies can distort your perception of price, making it difficult to compare products effectively. By looking at the price per unit, you can cut through the marketing noise and make the most economical choice.

"Spoilage" Alert:

Just because it's a good deal doesn't mean you should buy more than you need. Don't buy extra items with a short shelf life, such as perishables, since they can spoil quickly—ruining your potential savings along with them.

Auto Subscriptions

For products you purchase regularly, subscribe to companies that offer Auto Subscription discounts. Usually, these options will auto-ship your products on a certain date every month. In many cases, doing so will save you 10% or more on the purchase price. These savings can be quite considerable for something like cat litter or dog food. Other options for auto subscriptions may include products like health supplements, diapers, baby formula, and more.

Remember, be careful with subscriptions, which are often "forgotten" expenses. And don't change your buying behaviors just to get a discount. Otherwise, you will end up with more items than you need and more purchases than normal, which will throw off your monthly budget. Since these are paid and shipped automatically, remember that you are still subscribed (and don't forget to budget for them).

End of the Season Sales

High-end clothing and department stores like Nordstrom and Bloomingdale's will often have sales at the end of the season, where shoppers can save 20-40%. Waiting for Black Friday or other sales is a great way to save money on items you want without paying the sticker price. If you have the willpower to wait, you can often save hundreds of dollars. Similarly, we recommend purchasing birthday and holiday gifts throughout the year when they are on sale rather than waiting until the last minute. For example, Christmas cards and decorations are usually 50% off (or more) right after Christmas. Getting a good deal and saving money is a great way to get free money, even if it means hiding the gift in the closet for a few months.

Think Before Leasing a New Car

Regarding a car lease, review all the details. One recent example we came across was someone who had a car with a lease turn-in. The natural process would be to turn it in and get a new car/lease. However, in this particular case, our friend loved the car, which had low mileage. After researching, she realized she could pay off the car for $18,000, and the car's value, on the same day, was $25,000. While paying the $18,000 out of her emergency fund to buy the car was painful, she turned around and sold it for the Kelly Blue Book value. After selling her car, which took just a little more effort, her net assets improved by $7,000. Not a bad payday for a few hours of work! Sometimes, simple actions can really pay off. Remember, it's about staying in the habit of looking for "free money."

Have a System and Stick to It

Much of this advice may feel like common sense—but that's a good thing. If this chapter feels rudimentary, that's a sign that you are already good at managing your finances. It also is important wisdom to remember as you make more money. When you get a pay raise, it can be a great reward to start making some necessary upgrades to your life (in proportion to your new income) but be very careful. Make sure that these upgrades still keep you within the 50/20/30 budget plan. As your income grows, remember, your savings should also increase by the same amount because this money is technically "free." With a strong system in place, your monthly budget would account for this, and you would automatically start saving more toward retirement, expediting your climb toward financial freedom.

Simple Road Recap

In this chapter, we discussed where to find "free money."

Some of the top ideas:

1. Pick the right credit card. Finding one that pays 2% cash back is a game changer that can add up to more than $800 annually. Just make sure you don't increase your spending and put more items on your credit card to get more cash back.

2. Loyalty programs. Take advantage of money off your meals or purchases. Again, just make sure you don't change your buying habits in an attempt to acquire more loyalty points.

3. Be smart with your shopping and buy in bulk whenever possible. Just make sure you don't overbuy, especially with perishable items.

CHAPTER 12

Auto and Home/Renters Insurance

As you embark on the climb up the mountain, the higher you go, the more susceptible you are to accidents. Similarly, the more wealth you accumulate, the more you have to lose, and it becomes easier to make glaring errors and oversights, especially regarding insurance. Part of your preparation for becoming a millionaire should be thinking ahead about some of the things that will help you not only make money but keep it. Insurance is one of the necessary aspects of becoming a millionaire, ensuring you protect what you've worked so hard to earn. Whether it's your car, your apartment, your home, or even your life expectancy, it's crucial to ensure you are covered in case of an emergency. Think of it like the rope that keeps you tethered to the mountain. When you really need it, it's there for you.

We could write an entire book about life insurance and the differences in policies, but we will save that conversation for its own chapter in the next section of the book. For most people, auto and home/renters insurance will be two areas that can save you money while keeping you protected from pitfalls when you are new to the workforce. When you're just starting out, insurance may not seem like a big deal. If you're driving a fifteen-year-old car and total it in an accident, you're probably only out a couple of thousand dollars for the value of the vehicle. But as you earn more and start driving nicer cars, an accident could lead to costly repairs, higher insurance premiums, and money from Bucket 1 covering these increased expenses. They say that failing to plan is planning to fail, and this axiom is unequivocally true when it comes to insurance.

So, what's the big deal about insurance on the road toward financial freedom? Without realizing it, many people waste money on insurance by not taking the time to check for a few simple factors. We'll share a few of the heavy hitters with you in this chapter so you can leverage any additional savings toward your investments.

For most people, overpaying on insurance policies often occurs by carrying a low deductible for auto insurance and missing out on money-saving principles. Our perspective is that insurance is designed to be there in case of an emergency to fund a major, unexpected event. As such, we suggest having as high a deductible as you can manage, allowing for a lower annual premium. To understand your risk tolerance, answer this question: "If you were involved in an at-fault car accident and the damage was $1,000, would you file a claim, or would you pay it out of pocket?" Remember, filing a claim usually means your insurance rates will increase for 2 to 3 years. If you file a claim, you should probably opt for the highest deductible you feel comfortable with, even if that means paying a slightly higher premium.

This approach prevents you from incurring a large expense if you haven't saved enough for your emergency fund yet. However, if you have a fully funded emergency fund, you might want to consider raising your deductible to save money. Since the odds are low that you'll need it and that you'll actually file a claim in the event of an accident, you can select a higher deductible with a lower premium, investing the difference. For instance, saving $200 a year by choosing a higher deductible could be leveraged by investing it to earn returns. We typically recommend a deductible of $1,000 or higher, assuming you have that money in your emergency fund.

We also advocate for shopping around annually, obtaining at least three quotes from different insurance companies. Do your homework in advance and look for gaps in coverage. Don't wait to read the fine print until you need to file a claim. Remember, the cheapest insurance premium may not always be the best.

Prices can fluctuate yearly based on crime statistics or the number of accidents in your area. If pricing is comparable with other companies, it might be in your best interest to stay with your current provider, possibly benefiting from a "loyalty discount."

Sometimes, rates will skyrocket. If your policies are set to auto-renew (which often saves money), you might be surprised by new rates. If you have questions or don't understand something, ask your insurance company or agent. Consider the insurance company's price, service levels, and financial stability. We also suggest paying your premium in full to avoid finance charges. Since you'll be paying this bill anyway, it makes sense to pay upfront and save. We advise investing the difference. Another useful tip that could save you hundreds of dollars per year is combining your auto and home/renter's policies. By bundling these, insurance companies often pass more savings onto you.

Additionally, many people overlook that homeowners' insurance policies are often cheaper when a security system is in place. Sometimes, the savings over several years can justify installing a security system that, over time, pays for itself. Acquiring a "free" home security system just by thinking strategically about your insurance savings is a way to maximize the necessity of paying for insurance.

One way you can ensure you get the right coverage for your unique situation is to walk through some hypothetical scenarios with your agent to see what a claim would look like and to double-check that you are covered. For instance, if you live in a house with a basement that floods frequently, you will want to ask about what happens if you get heavy rains. What is covered? What is not covered? What out-of-pocket expenses are there? In the case of auto insurance, people often forget to ask about things like a cracked windshield. Usually, the agent can add coverage for just a few dollars a month to cover these types of costly repairs. But the key is to ask *before* committing to a policy.

Consumer credit score is another area that consumers often overlook when it comes to insurability. The higher your score, the lower your insurance premium rate often is. Keep in mind that many determining factors go into creating your rate. Often, the insurance company will conduct its own independent research, leveraging databases with multiple points of information—more than you provide—such as pulling your full credit report. It's important not to lie about any items on your policy. For instance, if you have a side hustle involving your car and get into an accident but never inform your insurance company, they may not cover your accident. If you have items in your home that you claimed you didn't, like a trampoline, the insurance company might not cover you. While you may save a few dollars in the short term, it can be much costlier if you lack coverage for a major emergency, such as a kitchen fire, the neighbor's child getting injured on your trampoline, or a totaled car used as a business vehicle.

Always look for discounts. Many insurance companies offer reductions based on alumni groups, membership clubs, and other affiliations. Don't forget to update your policy frequently. If you start working remotely and no longer commute to work, request a policy review. Ensure you have only the coverage you need and that you are protected so that if the unexpected occurs, you don't find yourself sliding down the financial mountain.

Simple Road Recap

In this chapter, we discussed auto and home/renters insurance.

Some key takeaways:

1. Think of your insurance as something to be used "only in an emergency."

2. You should go with as high of a deductible as possible. A $1,000 deductible vs. a $100 deductible can save you more than $500 annually.

3. Shop around yearly. Sometimes, you'll be surprised how rates can fluctuate from year to year.

PART 2

When Life Gets More Complicated

The Middle of the Climb: Mark's Journey

"I'd been climbing for days. My body ached everywhere. I had pain in muscles I didn't even know I had. At this point in the climb, the terrain was getting steeper, too, challenging not only my body but also my mindset. At the beginning of the climb, I was just taking a nice, casual stroll up the mountain, but now I was grinding my hands and feet into the sides of the rocks, clinging on for dear life thousands of feet above the ground. Every foot higher we climbed felt like an accomplishment. Things that I had taken for granted at the beginning of the climb, like changing elevation and temperature, were now becoming major considerations. There was no denying it—the climb had become more complicated than I had anticipated.

But just because it was hard didn't mean I wasn't up for the challenge. Hour after hour, I continued to push my mind, my body, and my spirit up the mountain. I had a clear goal in mind, and I knew I was going to make it to the top. I knew, deep down, that not every step of the journey would be fun and pain-free. But doing the work now would mean I could finally relax and enjoy the view when we got to the peak of our summit. At this elevation, any lost footing could be dangerous. I wanted to daydream about how nice it would feel to bask under the sunlight at the top of the mountain, but for now, I needed to focus on taking things one small step at a time."

"When Life Gets More Complicated" is the name of this section of the book, and for good reason. Once you start earning more, investing, getting married, and having children, there are more moving pieces involved in your financial puzzle. Just like Mark climbing the mountain, you need safety protocols in place for what will happen with your assets *before* you reach higher elevations; otherwise, the financial fallout could be disastrous. As such, in this part of the book, you will encounter several checkpoints where we will ask you to **Stop, Talk,** and **Listen**. You should **Stop** before making any major financial decisions, **Talk** to a qualified professional before taking action, and **Listen** to what they have to say. We will call these **STL CHECKPOINTS**. You can think of these as rest checkpoints along your climb. Even if you have the strength to keep climbing, sometimes it's best to pause first and get some rest and a new perspective before continuing.

CHAPTER 13

Your Silent Partner: Taxes and the IRS

Most climbers need a guide to help them navigate the unfamiliar, twisting terrain of the mountain. But what if your guide unexpectedly gives you an ultimatum? He's willing and able to guide you up the mountain on one condition—*his uncle wants to tag along.*

Internally, you're torn. You need the guide's help. In fact, without him, you won't be able to make the climb at all. But do you really want to spend your entire climb with another stranger—this guy named *Uncle Sam*? Let's pretend in this scenario that you have to bite your tongue and allow this tag-along to join you. (Oh, and the guide forgot to mention that his uncle has no equipment, food, or supplies, so he will share yours.) Relax; *Uncle Sam* will be right there every meal you eat, awkwardly waiting for you to give him his portion.

This partner is a metaphor for how most people view the IRS, or as some people still call them—*Uncle Sam*. While it may sound silly, *Uncle Sam* is trailing you every step up the mountain. Taxes may not seem like a huge deal when you are just starting out. However, as you start making your ascent up the financial mountain and earning more money, the IRS will become your silent business partner. The more you make, the more you'll pay in taxes. As life gets more complicated in your 30s and 40s, your tax bill will also likely be steeper. If you invest your money, finding ways to minimize how much you owe in taxes will become a higher priority for you because it will cut into your money.

Like it or not, you are being taxed when you make money, when your saved money grows, and in some cases, even when you die with money left in your portfolio. No matter how far you climb up the mountain, the IRS is there as your silent partner, following right behind you, waiting for their payment every step of the way. Don't believe us? There are numerous types of taxes you will encounter in your lifetime. Federal and state taxes, city tax, capital gains tax, property tax, self-employment tax, AMT (Alternative Minimum Tax) sales tax, gasoline tax, gift tax, auto registration tax, water and electrical taxes, cell phone tax, alcohol tax, cigarette tax, and marijuana tax—just to name a few.

We want you to take advantage of tax strategies that can be used for your benefit. Many people aren't aware of just how much you can do to help minimize the taxes you pay each year.

In this chapter, we're going to touch on a few key subjects:

IRS Overview
- Rewards and Penalties
- IRAs and 401(k)s
- Retirement Account Taxes - STL CHECKPOINT
- Deductions Matter
- Tax Brackets

Ways to Reduce Your Tax Bill
- Tax-Loss Harvesting/Wash Rule
- Charitable giving - Donor-Advised Funds

Rewards and Penalties

Human psychology is pretty simple. As a species, we like to maximize pleasure and minimize pain. The fact is that the government uses taxes both as a reward and a penalty, tapping into this great maxim of human psychology. The IRS motivates taxpayer behavior by rewarding people for doing what they want you to do—investing, taking business risks, hiring employees, etc. And it penalizes people for doing what they don't want you to do—consuming illicit substances, gambling, and not paying your taxes on time.

Penalties are put in place to discourage behavior, and rewards are there to incentivize it. Rental depreciation is a great example of how the government encourages you to take the risk to make investments. You can write off a rental property's qualifying expenses for years to potentially save on your yearly tax bill. The government knows that real estate is an important part of our economy, and they encourage people to take risks and to be invested in the market. So, what do they do to motivate you to behave this way? They give you a tax break for rental depreciation to entice this behavior. And for most real estate investors, it is a welcome reward they gladly take advantage of every year.

But what about every time you buy a pack of cigarettes, a handheld vape pen, cannabis, or alcohol? The government taxes it at an incredibly high rate—much higher than your average sales tax. Why? Because the government possibly wants to discourage you from partaking in risky behaviors that will most likely cost *them* money in the long run. Think about it: if you aren't healthy enough to earn a high income year after year and pay your taxes, they lose money. The longer you live and the healthier you are, the more tax you will most likely pay over your lifetime. Likewise, if you end up with costly surgeries and hospital stays in your later years, Medicare may have to foot the bill, costing the government money.

Many people don't put a lot of thought into how much they are actually being taxed. On *The Simple Road Toward Financial Freedom,* the goal is to pay the exact amount you owe. Not a penny more, and not a penny less. You can send the government a tip as a thank-you if you want, but you don't have to. It may sound silly to think about tipping the IRS, but when you overpay on your tax bill, that's exactly what you are doing. Savvy investors do everything they can to maximize the money they save on taxes.

Remember the famous words of Benjamin Franklin when he said, "In this world, nothing is certain but death and taxes."

IRAs, 401(k)s, and HSAs

Let's revisit one of the most important aspects of taxes for a moment: the taxes imposed on your retirement accounts. When it comes to retirement accounts, we suggest you max out your contributions to take full advantage of the money-saving tax benefits that the IRS offers.

Retirement Account Taxes - <u>STL CHECKPOINT</u>

When you are just starting on your journey up the mountain, the important thing is that you get into the habit of putting money toward your retirement savings. Thinking about the taxes you must pay in retirement isn't as important as being diligent about saving consistently. But as you get higher up the mountain and you start to get a clearer picture of your financial situation and what your future needs will be for your family, it may be a good time to stop and reevaluate. You can get gratification now by saving on taxes today, like in a traditional IRA or 401(k). However, in retirement, you will eventually have to pay the taxes on your investment.

Some people are best served by a Roth IRA or Roth 401(k), where they will pay taxes upfront today (by using income that has already been taxed) so that they pay taxes on the smaller amount instead of paying on the total accumulation of their account in retirement. But remember, you won't be investing as much since you're paying with after-tax dollars. Others will benefit from a traditional IRA, 401(k), or other employer-sponsored retirement plan, where they benefit from deducting these contributions (or paying with pre-tax dollars) from that year's taxes.

Knowing which retirement account tax strategy is right for you and your unique needs is an art form, not an exact science. It would be nice if one was clearly better than the other, but like all things financial, there are tradeoff decisions that you must take into account for your unique situation. For most people, funding both types of accounts is a suitable strategy. As you accumulate wealth, you may want to talk with a professional.

Deductions Matter

One of the ways that the IRS helps you lower your tax burden is by a process called deductions. Deductions *lower* your MAGI (Modified Adjusted Gross Income) or the amount subject to taxes. The more deductions you take, the less you will owe because deductions effectively reduce your taxable income. However, it's important to remember that deductions aren't 100% free.

Deductions come in two different forms: itemized deductions and standardized deductions. But for most people, depending on your unique situation, the standard deduction will be most applicable. Remembering to take that deduction can be a significant way to lower your bill. You can also itemize deductions, which means adding up expenses. The standard deduction is a lump sum deduction that everyone can take advantage of that will *significantly lower your tax bill, even if you don't have any expenses.*

Tax Brackets

A big misconception is that if you make more money, *all* of your money will now be taxed at the *highest* tax bracket you enter into. It's not.

Let's look at some 2024 numbers to help explain how deductions work for you to help lower your tax bill.

"I Don't Want to Make Any More Money Because I'll Pay More in Taxes"

- 37% for incomes over $609,351 ($731,201 for married couples filing jointly).
- 35% for incomes over $243,726 ($487,451 for married couples filing jointly).
- 32% for incomes over $191,951 ($383,901 for married couples filing jointly).
- 24% for incomes over $100,526 ($201,051 for married couples filing jointly).
- 22% for incomes over $47,151 ($94,301 for married couples filing jointly).
- 12% for incomes over $11,601 ($23,201 for married couples filing jointly).
- 10% for incomes of single individuals with incomes of $11,600 or less ($23,200 for married couples filing jointly).[17]

For example, if you make $50,000 per year, you would be in the 22% bracket, but only $5,275 is taxed at 22%. The rest would be taxed at 12% and 10%, respectively. (It's important to remember that the tax code is constantly changing, so these numbers will move up and down year-to-year.) Even Warren Buffett only pays 10% on the first $11,600 he makes—just like everyone else.

For most people, the standard deduction will be the most applicable deduction you can use to lower your tax bill. It's important to make sure that you claim it, especially if you file your own tax return using software such as

---

[17] IRS provides tax inflation adjustments for tax year 2024 | Internal Revenue Service. Author: IRS, *IRS Provides Tax Inflation Adjustments for tax year 2024*, 11/9/23.

TurboTax to e-file. The standard deduction is $14,600 for 2024 and $29,200 for married couples filing jointly. So, at an income of $50,000 per year—a single person would only be paying taxes on $35,400 after the standard deduction.

But what about itemized deductions?

The most common itemized deductions are things like *property taxes, mortgage interest, donations to charities, sales taxes, and medical and dental expenses (if the medical expenses exceed 7.5% of your income).* These types of things (for the majority of people) don't add up to over $14,600 for a single person or $29,200 for married couples. That's why most people end up taking the standard deduction. If your itemized deductions are going to tally up to a number that is close to the standard deduction, you may want to take the time to run the numbers and see which number is higher.

Tax Credits vs. Tax Deductions

Often, you'll hear about tax credits and tax deductions. Keep in mind, if you receive what's known as a "tax credit," that is much better than a "deduction." A deduction saves you a percentage of the dollar amount you deduct by reducing your taxable income, but a tax credit is dollar-for-dollar, the exact amount of money that will go back into your pocket.

Ways to Reduce Your Tax Bill

Tax-Loss Harvesting

Tax-loss harvesting is the timely selling of securities at a loss to offset the amount of capital gains tax owed from selling profitable assets. Tax-loss harvesting allows you to offset your realized gain with a realized loss by selling the stock, so you end up paying less in taxes.

For example, if you sell a stock in a single year with a long-term capital gain, you can then look for opportunities in your portfolio to sell a stock with a loss. The net difference, if a gain, will be taxed. If you realize more losses than gains, the difference can be carried forward to future tax years. This is known as "carry forward" losses and is a very effective way to reduce your tax liability. Just remember, a "wash rule" goes into effect if you repurchase the investment within 30 days. (Be careful to follow the rules and talk with your CPA or accountant if you have any questions.)

Here is a simple example:

You own ten shares of ABC company. You purchased the shares for $100 per share, which are now worth $200 per share. When you sell, you will have a $1,000 capital gain and must pay taxes on the gain.

You also own ten shares of XYZ company. You purchased the shares shortly before the stock market went down. You bought the shares at $200 per share, which are now worth $100 per share. You have a $1,000 capital loss on this investment.

If you made these moves, your loss would offset your capital gain, and you would not owe tax on your capital gain. With the wash rule, you need to make sure you don't purchase XYZ company within 30 days of selling it for a loss.

Charitable Giving

When you donate to charity, the IRS rewards you for being generous. It is also a great way to give back, and support causes you care about and help those less fortunate. You can give more than just cash; you can also give securities (stocks/bonds, etc.). This gives investors the benefit of a potential tax deduction. Now, charitable donations are typically only for taxpayers who itemize their deductions since donations are capped when you take a standard deduction. The IRS rewards you in a few ways depending on how you donate to charities.

Cash Donations

When you donate cash, you can subtract your donation from your taxable income. For example, if you make a $2,000 donation, you can deduct that $2,000 from your taxable income, but *only if you elect to itemize your deductions.*

Securities

For donated securities, you can deduct the value of the securities (stocks, bonds, etc.) at the time of the donation, including any capital gains. For example, imagine you have ten shares of XYZ company worth $2,000 ($200 per share). When you purchased those shares, you bought them for $1,500 ($150 per share). Under normal circumstances, you would owe a capital gain tax on the $500 you made when you sold the shares. However, if you choose to donate the shares instead, you can deduct the entire $2,000 from your taxable income so that you do not have to pay capital gains taxes.

Donor-Advised Funds

Another type of specialized charitable deduction that works as a great tax vehicle is called a Donor-Advised Fund (DAF). DAFs allow you to write off charitable contributions. But there's a catch. A donor-advised fund is essentially an account where you put money that can *only* be used for donating to charities. Once you place the money into a DAF, there's no pulling it out. It *must* go to a charitable organization, but there is no stipulation on when you must donate the money or which charities you must donate the money to, as long as it is a qualifying 501(c)(3). Donor-Advised Funds are sometimes referred to as "Giving Accounts" because when you donate to your Giving Account, you can take the same tax deductions as if you were donating to any public charity.

The strategic advantage of a DAF is that once it's funded, you don't have to donate it all at once or to just one charity. It allows you to disburse the money as you see fit. You can also invest the assets in the fund into something like an index fund or mutual fund so that the account has the chance to appreciate in value, and the beauty of a DAF is that you don't have to pay capital gains taxes and/or ordinary income taxes on any appreciation.

The big benefit to taxpayers is that donating through a DAF allows you to potentially write off whatever money you invest into the account in the year you allocate funds to the DAF. That means you can invest the money in different charities over time, but you still get the tax benefits of a big write-off in the year you move money from your portfolio into the DAF. Remember, once you put money into this fund—it's gone. You can't get it back, but you can control how you use it and which charitable organizations it goes to. Just make sure to choose a DAF with a low fee structure. Some financial services firms like Vanguard or Schwab will require a minimum deposit amount to open a DAF account, but at firms like Fidelity, there is no minimum, but there might be administrative and investment fees attached, so you'll want to do your homework.

When you are looking for an opportunity to reduce your taxes and you have a high income, a DAF can be a fantastic strategy. Talk to a professional to help you out. A lot of Mark's clients will look ahead and do a little financial forecasting to see when they will have a big tax bill due. Then, they strategically "bunch" their charitable giving into one year to get a larger deduction in that year, which lowers their large bill.

Tax Laws Are Constantly Changing

Does tax season get you down, thinking about all that money that could be going into your pocket? Long before Ronald Reagan took up his post in the Oval Office as President of the United States, he was a Hollywood actor. Back in his day, his friends in Hollywood often heard him commenting that he could only star in two movies per year. Why? He had no economic incentive to do a third movie because the third movie would put him in the highest tax bracket, where 90% of his earnings would go to taxes! Today, 90% sounds extreme, but back then, for high-income individuals, it was a fact of life.

Remember, the tax rates are always subject to change. Our point in mentioning this is that if we knew what the tax code will be for the next 30–35 years, and we knew what your income was going to be, we could tell you *exactly* what to do for retirement planning. But since no one has a crystal ball to predict the future, all we can do is plan for today and assume everything will go forward as planned. If something changes, we make changes.

As you plan for your retirement and try to reduce your future tax bills, we think it's safe to plan on taxes staying the same or going up. If we're wrong and taxes go down, then everyone is happy. But if you bet on them to go down and they go up, it can impact your net worth. Being strategic about taxes can speed up your road toward financial freedom. If you plan ahead for them, you can maximize your deductions and minimize your tax burden.

Simple Road Recap

In this chapter, we discussed the silent partner in our financial journey—the IRS. We also mentioned that as things become more complicated, you need to take "Stop, Talk, and Listen" moments. This section had our first <u>STL CHECKPOINT</u>. It's also critical to take advantage of the many tax-saving vehicles the IRS allows, like deductions, a Donor-Advised Fund, and tax-loss harvesting.

CHAPTER 14

Assets vs. Liabilities

Let's talk about one of the most important skill sets you can develop to help you fast-track your climb up the financial mountain.

Nearly every object you buy in your *wants* category (30% of your monthly budget) can be split into two categories: *assets* and *liabilities*. Making the distinction between the two is an area of money management where many people slip up. Not being able to distinguish between these two categories can cost them their financial freedom and potentially cause them to cascade away from their goals and backslide down the mountain. Below is a quick definition of these two vital financial terms, as we see it with a slightly different example. Your ability to distinguish between them is one of the most important tools at your disposal as an aspiring millionaire.

An **asset** should *appreciate* (go up) in value or *hold value* (stay the same).

A **liability** should *depreciate* (go down) in value.

Reread those definitions again because this is really pivotal to your financial well-being in our opinion. Many people really need to look in the mirror and ask themselves if they truly understand this point. An easy litmus test you can conduct to find out if your purchase is an asset or a liability is to ask yourself, "Two years from now, is this item going to be the same value, go up in value, or will it be worth less than what I bought it for?" For the majority of purchases you will make in your life—furniture, clothing, food, fun, entertainment, toys, vehicles, etc.—the answer will be the latter. Even though you typically need these items to live, they likely won't go up in value, so they technically won't be considered assets. If you treat it as a liability and it becomes an asset—that's great. But don't fool yourself.

The wealthy focus on acquiring assets, while the herd acquires liabilities that *look* like assets. Let's dive into a few examples of liabilities vs. assets to uncover the mystery behind the two and see what this looks like in real life.

Assets

Retirement Funds
Any money you have invested in 401(k), 403(b), Roth, IRA, or HSA are considered assets. These will most likely appreciate over time.

Investment Funds
Stocks, ETFs, Mutual Funds, Bonds, CDs, and high-yield savings accounts are all examples of investments that will likely appreciate in the long term.

Education
Having a formal education can be an asset if it helps you earn more money.

Real Estate / Rental Properties / Family Home
Real estate and rental properties can be great assets and income sources for generating monthly cash flow. But just like with education, there are downsides to these types of large purchases. Market fluctuations, changing neighborhoods, property taxes, and upkeep can turn a real estate investment into an expensive liability if you aren't careful.

Liabilities

Automobiles

A timeless adage is that new cars lose 10% of their value when they drive off the lot. Generally speaking, cars lose value each year. However, reliable transportation is essential to be safe and arrive at work on time.

Vacations

From a financial standpoint, vacations can be a financial drain. However, vacations can be helpful and even necessary in some cases to allow you to de-stress and gain perspective on your life. They give you an Emotional ROI, not necessarily a Financial ROI.

Credit Cards and Other High-Interest Debt

Credit cards may seem like a saving grace when you are short on cash, but at upwards of 20% yearly APR at the time of this writing, they make little sense on paper. Debt starts adding up very quickly, and bad money habits like overspending on credit cards can be incredibly tempting.

Not Planning for Taxes

If you are strategic about your tax bill, you should be able to take advantage of several deductions to lower the amount you owe. However, if you don't plan ahead, you may be stuck with a large, unexpected bill that can really hurt your budget.

Stuff—Clothes, Collectibles, Electronics

Today's high-tech latest and greatest (fill in the blank here) is tomorrow's junk. Yard sales, vintage stores, and Facebook Marketplace are filled with people trying to get rid of these liabilities, or what most people would call "junk."

So, what does this mean?

At first glance, many of the liabilities listed above may seem like perfectly natural expenses. After all, your family needs a car, right? And your children need toys, don't they? While these are valid points, the problem isn't that people buy houses, cars, or toys for their children. The problem is when people buy liabilities while believing that they are actually purchasing assets.

So, why do so many people fall into the trap of buying liabilities that are disguised as assets? There are lots of reasons people do this. In fact, it's pretty rampant in our Instagram-obsessed culture. Fancy destination vacations, flashy cars, expensive jewelry, and designer clothes look good online, and they are quick ways to make new friends and show off. But be careful with thinking these types of expenses will make you rich. Remember, whenever you buy a liability, the real cost isn't the price tag or the MSRP sticker price. You have lost out on putting that money to work for you in the stock market or another investment vehicle where that money has the chance to be an asset and grow.

Frequently, when someone inherits money or wins a lot of money, the first thing they do is upgrade their car and their TV. These are both great examples of depreciating assets. (When was the last time you were in the "used TV" market? Probably never.)

You may be wondering, *Why have we been taught to prioritize buying liabilities over assets?* A lot of people have a "life is short" mentality. They want to reward themselves—and there's nothing wrong with that. But if you would like to be on the fast path to financial freedom (and most people sincerely do), you must prioritize buying assets, saving, and investing your money first. Then, you can buy flashy liabilities and not worry about the price tag.

Financing

One important caveat to this conversation about liabilities and assets is the concept of financing. *A good rule of thumb is to pay cash (or pay it off in 30 days) for all the toys in your life: a 4-wheeler, boat, motorcycle, etc.* When you finance liabilities, you are paying interest on something that is most likely losing value—while the creditor is making money off of your monthly interest payments. However, if you finance assets that *earn* you money, you can potentially make money while you are paying off their principal cost. Eventually, you may even earn regular cash flow from them once the financing period ends. This is a smart strategy to build wealth. But always remember that the devil is in the details.

Simple Road Recap

In this chapter, we focused on assets vs. liabilities. Our definition of assets are things that appreciate (grow) in value, while liabilities depreciate (lose value). The goal was to help you think about these things before making a purchase. The more you can purchase assets instead of liabilities, the quicker you'll get on *The Simple Road Toward Financial Freedom*.

CHAPTER 15

"But It's Only $400 per Month"

You've probably seen one of your friends showing off a new, expensive purchase. Whether it's a brand-new Audi, a big-screen TV, or flashy designer clothing, it might be hard to understand how your friend, who isn't a millionaire, can afford a luxury item. When asked, they'll often spill the beans (they are your friend, after all) and explain their secret: *special 0% introductory APR financing*. At that moment, your friend is delighted with their new purchase. They have the newest car, hot off the lot, and the best part is their financing is dirt cheap. While the purchase may be a financial setback, it makes you wonder what you could afford.

Six months later, you are out with a large group of friends (including the friend who bought the new car). Out of nowhere, they reach across the table to pick up the tab. They graciously offer to pay for dinner for the entire table. You're shocked. The bill is $400 after dinner, a few rounds of drinks, and a generous tip. "Don't mention it," they say as they slide their shiny new American Express card into the black plastic card slot. Your friend leans in and whispers, "Don't worry. I have a 15-month 0% APR on my new card. It's like free money."

You can probably guess where this story is going. The problem with these enticing financing offers is that most people don't use them *just once*. While

MARK SCHLIPMAN & STEVE SHORT

financing a big-screen TV or car and taking advantage of special introductory interest rates can be a good idea (when used sparingly), the problem is when people abuse these offers. Their eyes are bigger than their bank accounts, and money quickly goes out the door without them realizing it.

The Psychology of Monthly Payments

A funny thing happens psychologically when people start paying for large purchases over time. Instead of recognizing that they pay every dollar on the price tag of a $36,000 new car, the salesman asks them how much they can afford *per month*. This question starts turning the wheels of debt in their head long before they sign on the dotted line. As if by magic, they realize that they could probably pay more than they originally had guessed. The car with the $36,000 price tag only costs $500 a month, but they could afford almost twice that! Suddenly, the salesman whisks them over to their dream car with a sticker price of $72,000 for just $1,000-$1,500 a month (for 72 months); they can drive the car of their dreams today! Here's the problem—a 72-month car loan will accrue an astronomical amount of interest over time. Before they know it, they've just signed away $12,000 of debt (plus interest) per year for the next six years. They forget all about the fact that they are spending $36,000 more than they budgeted. Instead, they only focus on the fact that it is only about $500 more per month.

As we've already shared, the danger of financing isn't usually the first purchase you make. The real threat is that it can lead to budget creep. It's the gift that keeps on giving in the form of yearly interest and payments that can really add up. Remember your hypothetical friend who paid for a night out on the town because it was "only $400"? Be extremely careful with statements like this. The average worker in the United States can afford a $400 per month expense on a credit card, but the real cost isn't just $400. It's $400 x multiple months. One year of spending $400 monthly on unnecessary purchases would be $4,800 (plus interest). Over two years, it would be $9,600. It adds up quickly. That extra $5k or $10k per year could be going toward a retirement account, a child's college savings fund, or paying down a mortgage. Instead, it often goes toward superfluous expenses like going out to eat at expensive restaurants, taking trips to exotic locales, or impressing your friends by posting your new stuff on social media—all liabilities, not assets. There's nothing wrong with having a mortgage payment and a car payment. Most people can't afford to pay cash for their house or their car.

Delayed Gratification

Delayed gratification is one of the most important aspects of financial planning. If you can learn to maintain a consistent budget for the first few years of your working life, you will be less susceptible to budget creep. Just as scientists have discovered that those who don't smoke before the age of 30 will likely never start, the same logic applies to your financial habits. Many people who start earning more money start spending more money. We've made this point several times throughout this book already, but for good reason. It is a very common ailment on the American financial health continuum. Most people don't want to delay gratification to have a little less today so they can have twice as much tomorrow. Instead, they place unnecessary pressure on their future selves by wanting more today and having to pay it back tomorrow. If you have the disposable income to buy something and pay cash, do it. But we would not recommend financing.

Every expense you finance today will become tomorrow's debt. Before financing anything, ask yourself, do I really want to be paying this off years from now? Sticking to the budget you set in Chapter 2 may not seem like a big deal. But what most people fail to see is that sticking to a budget is a *financial superpower*. When you commit to a budget and stick to it over time, that's when you see the long-term results of your efforts. Just like committing to going to the gym the first few months, you may not notice a huge difference, but if you commit every day for a year or two and stick to the plan, you can transform your health, physique, and fitness level. The same is true with your financial health. It all comes down to your mindset. How consistently can you do the little things right over a long period? Remember, if you stick to the budget, you don't have to invest as much. Investing a little bit today is "cheaper" than investing a lot more later.

Think long and hard, and we would recommend even "sleeping" on it before you ever finance anything. Make sure, if you pull the trigger, you really should do it. Ask yourself: *Will this new monthly obligation create additional stress in my life?* Most financial stressors are self-induced by choice. It may not cause you any stress right now, but monthly payments and high-interest rates could cause you unnecessary stress for the next 3 to 5 years.

It's empowering when you look at an advertisement or commercial to think to yourself, "How is this company trying to get me to spend money?" Buying the next thing may make you happy right now because it gives you a nice dopamine boost, but there's no guarantee that you'll still be excited about your purchase six weeks from now. If you finance, the only thing that is guaranteed is that you'll still be paying off that purchase.

Don't fall in love with a monthly payment amount.

Ask yourself: *In three years, will I still be excited about this purchase, even though I'm still sending the company a check every month to pay off this item?*

The larger the transaction, the longer you should spend on analyzing how this purchase fits into your financial plan. Train yourself to stay committed to your budget and your savings goals. It may take you a while, but once you make your way up the side of the mountain and catch that first glimpse of the horizon, you'll be glad you have the number saved in your portfolio much more than if you had a new car parked in your driveway. Financial freedom comes at a price. Some people will trade their financial freedom for a liability. Others will reap the long-term rewards of being financially stress-free.

Simple Road Recap

In this chapter, we discussed the mindset of "it's only $400 per month" and how it can lead to long-term issues. In summary, we suggest paying cash (or paying off your credit card immediately) for most purchases. When you think, *It's only $xx per month,* it tends to cause you to spend more money and ultimately set you up for the next 3 to 5 years with payments that can break your budget.

CHAPTER 16

Retirement Plans and Changes in Employment

The average worker will change jobs 12 times in their lifetime.[18] Let's put that into perspective for a moment. We will use a quick story to illustrate what this might look like.

Freshly minted with a new college degree, you start rapid-fire sending in applications, hoping to land your first salaried job. When you finally ace your interviews, you are elated. But about a year into your employment, you start casually browsing sites like LinkedIn and Glassdoor, quickly realizing you could get a nice, healthy salary bump if you took a role at a new company now that you have a little experience. So, you migrate to a new role, learn to adapt, and add valuable new skills to your tool belt. Your manager takes notice and offers you a promotion. With the promotion comes a nice salary raise. You are happy for a couple of years, but then you hear about an opportunity that offers more control over your workload with increased responsibility. So, you pack up shop and set sail for a new destination—a chance to, once again, improve your skill sets, earn more money, and keep climbing up the financial mountain.

---

[18] https://www.zippia.com/advice/average-number-jobs-in-lifetime/. Author: Chris Kolmar, *Average Number of Jobs in a Lifetime*, 1/11/23.

Every few years, you play this game—landing a job, securing benefits, waiting for a raise, and then, when you can, you jump ship and try to land a better role with a new company. Welcome to the 21st century. Gone are the days of everyone getting the "gold watch" at your company's retirement party when you decide to hang it up after 40 years on the job and trade a paycheck for a pension.

For most of you reading this book, job changes could be fast and frequent. The stage has been set for the possibility of more virtual and remote positions being filled, meaning you're competing for roles on a global scale since you may no longer need to live in the city where your company is based. It's also not unreasonable to change careers and industries at least once in your life. While you don't need to hang on to your job forever, you will want to hang onto all that money sitting in your old employer's retirement account. So, what do you do when you change jobs? Where does all that money go?

The good news is that even though you quit or get fired, your money in your 401(k), 403(b), and HSA doesn't disappear. If this has stopped you from enrolling in your workplace retirement plans in the past, don't make this common mistake. Your contribution will always remain yours.

Your Retirement Savings and Changes in Employment

If you are wondering what to do with your 401(k) or other employer-sponsored retirement plan, and your biggest concern is how to continue *deferring your taxes* into the future—congratulations! You are thinking just like a trained financial advisor. Sometimes, retirement plan savings can stay in a previous employer's plan. Other times, your money can't stay in the plan, and you need to take action, or your employer may move your money. The circumstances depend on the type of plan the employer offers and the amount of money you have in your account. The first thing you will want to do is to compare your options.

Cash Out or Rollover Money Out of Your Employer's Plan - STL CHECKPOINT

When you leave your employer, there are many choices regarding what to do with the money invested in your old company's retirement plan. As we've said before, the devil is in the details. Mixing pre-tax and after-tax retirement accounts may be more complicated than simply rolling over an employer's 401(k) plan. That's why this is a pivotal *Stop, Talk,* and *Listen Checkpoint* that can set you up for future success. The big takeaway that we want you to remember is that you have options to get your money into a new account, and if you do it correctly, you won't have to pay any taxes or penalties.

<u>Whatever you do, if you are thinking of cashing out—STOP!</u>

Do not cash out your employer-sponsored retirement plan without speaking to a professional first. This needs to be treated as an absolute last resort. There are steep penalties and tax implications, and the lost growth is irreversible. Cashing out is the equivalent of an avalanche tumbling toward you on the mountain. Do not do it.

Rollover into an Individual Retirement Account[19]

Rollovers can be a helpful strategy to use for any employer retirement account plan, such as 401(k), 403(b), PSPs, Roth 401(k), SIMPLE, and SEP IRA. Rollover is a term that means leaving the money in a retirement account but switching it from your employer's retirement account into either *your own personal account* or *a new employer's account.* <u>A rollover is not the same as a cash out.</u>

---

[19] Before deciding whether to retain assets in a 401(k) or roll over to an IRA, an investor should consider various factors including, but not limited to, investment options, fees and expenses, services, withdrawal penalties, protection from creditors and legal judgments, required minimum distributions and possession of employer stock. Please view the Investor Alerts section of the FINRA website for additional information.

There are some good reasons to choose a rollover to get that money out of your old employer's account and into your own Individual Retirement Account. When you choose to rollover retirement savings directly from one retirement plan into an IRA, there are no penalties or taxes. All of your money keeps working for you with tax advantages. This makes it easier to keep track of your money. You know where the money is, you know how it's invested, and you can easily rebalance investments or make other changes. But if you simply cash out, you will likely have to pay steep penalties and taxes on that money, so it is usually much smarter to perform a rollover instead. But there are also a few other other reasons you may want to consider a rollover.

Consolidating Retirement Accounts

You can do this to consolidate accounts. For example, if you have a Schwab investment account and an employer's retirement plan, you can create a new account and rollover your prior employer's retirement plan to Schwab to help keep things organized. One reason this is a common strategy is that rollovers, which help you consolidate your retirement accounts, can reduce the amount you pay in fees. Often, the fees associated with your employer's retirement account are paid by your employer. But when you are no longer employed, those fees/expenses typically get passed on to you.

Open Up More Investment Options

You may also want to do a rollover to open up more investment options. In many cases, employer-sponsored accounts have limited investment options. Maybe you only have 20 mutual funds to choose from in your employer's retirement plan vs. an Individual Retirement Account, which would give you more options. Having the freedom to invest in any mutual fund, ETF, stock, or bond could be a game changer for you in your ascent up the mountain.

Pre-Tax Funds vs. After-Tax Funds

Before you decide to rollover your employer-sponsored plan, make sure you know how much of your money is pre-tax and after-tax. For example, if you had a Roth 401(k), you would not want to roll your Roth 401(k) to a regular IRA because you would lose the tax-saving advantages of a Roth. Instead, you should roll the Roth 401(k) to your individual Roth IRA to continue receiving those tax benefits. But there are nuances to every situation, so this is something that you will want to discuss with a tax professional.[20]

$$401(k) \longrightarrow IRA$$
$$Roth\ 401(k) \longrightarrow Roth\ IRA$$

Rollover Your Old Employer's Plan into a New Employer's Plan

In some cases, you may want to simply rollover your old employer's retirement plan into your new employer's plan. For some situations, this may make a lot of sense. As mentioned above, another factor you may want to consider is the number of investment options available to you in your new employer's plan.

Remember that plans are not perfect. Mistakes can happen by plan administrators with 401(k) redemption and rollover requests. If you get a check made out to you personally from a 401(k), *don't cash it.* **You need to potentially redo your paperwork and get that money back into a 401(k) plan within a very short time window.**

---

[20] Distributions from traditional IRAs and employer sponsored retirement plans are taxed as ordinary income and, if taken prior to reaching age 59½, may be subject to an additional 10% IRS tax penalty. A Roth retirement account offers tax-free withdrawals on taxable contributions. To qualify for the tax-free and penalty-free withdrawal of earnings, a Roth account must be in place for at least five tax years, and the distribution must take place after age 59½, or due to death or disability. Depending on state law, Roth accounts distributions may be subject to state taxes.

Net Unrealized Appreciation

Some companies offer the benefit of employees owning stock in the employer company. The net unrealized appreciation is the difference in the value between the average cost basis of shares of employer stock and the current market value of the shares. The NUA (Net Unrealized Appreciation) is important if you are distributing highly appreciated employer stock from your employer-sponsored retirement plan.

Take Action

The reality is that financial decisions often inspire inertia. Another way to describe this is *analysis paralysis*. It can be tough to try to take autonomy over your financial destiny. Instead, it's easier to do nothing than to gather the information needed to make a confident decision. As a result, many people leave their retirement savings in former employers' plans.

Changing employment can be exciting, but it often comes with added stress. Do yourself a favor and take the extra stress and guesswork out of what to do next with your retirement account by exploring the options above to see what's right for your situation. Even if you've forgotten about your retirement account with your former employer, it is still worth doing the legwork to access your accounts. After all, it is *your money*!

Simple Road Recap:

In this chapter, we explained a few options for managing your employer-sponsored retirement plan after a job loss. We defined rollovers and explained how to rollover your employer-sponsored retirement funds into an Individual Retirement Account or your new employer's retirement plan. We also discussed a few nuances to remember, especially long-term tax-planning strategies.

CHAPTER 17

The Family Budget

Periodically, on your climb, you will need to stop and take inventory of your remaining supplies. Many new climbers quickly burn through their food, water, and other precious resources after the first night. Since climbing requires a lot of energy, it's critical that you are always aware of the resources available in your pack. If you want to reach the summit, you need a plan. Every ounce in your pack adds weight, costing you in the form of achy backs, sore knees, and increased energy exertion. This situation sets off a domino effect, making you consume more food to fuel your body due to the higher daily calorie burn. Sometimes, sacrifices are necessary to reach your goal. Remember, there is no magic vending machine waiting at the mountain's peak. Instead, you must be diligent about sticking to your plan, especially when other climbers depend on you.

Throughout this book, we've referred several times to the budget you created in Chapter 2. But what happens when life changes, such as getting married or having children, come along? Welcome to the family budget.

In this chapter, we will revisit your budget items from Chapter 2 and give them a facelift to accommodate some of the average American family household's monthly expenses. As your family grows, it's not just the size of your car or house that needs to expand—your expenses will increase as well.

More family members mean more mouths to feed, more clothes to purchase, and other incidentals that you may not have previously considered. Now is the perfect time to stop and take inventory before you and your partner start climbing at higher elevations.

A family brings more responsibility, including deciding how to manage your family's savings to ensure everyone's happiness and health for years to come. Having a family and getting married isn't for everyone. However, if this path applies to you—or you think it might one day—we encourage you to read this chapter.

Marrying Your Finances

Marriage isn't just about marrying two people; you also marry your finances. Part of coming together in marriage is looking at all of your assets and liabilities to determine who has what. It is essential to talk about finances *before* you get married. Unfortunately, it is hard enough for families to talk with children about money, let alone a new spouse. However, having a plan of attack can make the conversation a bit easier.

We suggest having an honest, open, and frank discussion about finances. Now's not the time to hold back on your thoughts and your feelings. Share all of your income and debts with your partner. When you are married, you will both be potentially taking them on together, regardless, so having the conversation now will only help prepare both of you. This might be a great conversation leading to increased encouragement, support, and even financial breakthroughs like paying debts faster. Being upfront with your income and debts before walking down the aisle is always better than surprising your partner on the honeymoon!

Your Family is a Small Business

One of the smartest ways to approach the family budget is to start thinking about your family as a small business. At the end of the day, you and your spouse (and eventually, your children) will be making decisions about what is important enough to invest in as a family. Treating these decisions like business decisions will help make compromises and tough choices easier. Viewing your family's financial situation in this light will help remove emotional barriers that can hinder financial progress.

Creating the family budget is an art form, not an exact science. There is no one-size-fits-all for financial risk tolerance. Instead, approach this conversation with your partner as a give-and-take. Be willing to *compromise* with your partner to meet your goals. One way to do this is to complete a risk tolerance questionnaire. This will help you to get clearer on where your partner is at with some of the big-picture financial decisions that affect marriages. It offers a time to discuss disagreements and work out a compromise ahead of time so that you both are on the same page moving forward.

It's important to ask some identifying questions to help guide your thinking on budget creation before you get married. Find out what types of money habits you and your partner have. Talk about what you value spending money on and be proactive about communicating your needs and compromising to meet their needs. Ask yourself: *Are you a spender or a saver? Where are your finances right now? In the past five years, have I been moving closer to financial freedom or further from it?*

Often, couples can be well-served to set a spending threshold to discuss with the other partner before making large purchases. Sometimes, the dopamine rush of impulsive "retail therapy" can make you forget all about your budget. Having a plan in place to consult your partner can help you to stay on track financially and not fall victim to impulsive spending. You can try setting a threshold for these items, such as any purchases over $100 must be a "team decision."

Make sure that you have important conversations about work-life balance before tying the knot. Designate roles for who will manage what. Talk about hypotheticals, like what would happen if one partner lost a job or couldn't return to work. Having these conversations can be a good way to grow closer with your partner and learn about their financial risk tolerance levels. Create clear and distinct roles. Don't delegate everything to one person. This is a recipe for resentment! If you decide to have a partner stay at home and take care of the kids, make sure that there is an appropriate balance between partners in other areas. Communicating about the different roles in the family "business" will help you to plan for the future together. When kids and elderly parents enter the picture, it can be a drain on finances. Communicate about important issues, such as a parent or post-college-aged child moving back in with you. Make sure that you plan well in advance of these life-changing transitions, as they can put a damper on your financial goals. Financial goal setting is incredibly important and often can get overlooked with the onslaught of to-do list items that begin popping up after you "pop the question." Financial planning shouldn't stop after you've saved up enough for the ring or the wedding—it is a lifelong venture.

Together, or Separate?

When you get married, one of the most important financial conversations you can have is deciding if you want to commingle your finances. Your union will likely mean combining two incomes to create one household income. That means that you and your spouse can create what is known as a *joint bank account*, where you can both have access to funds in the account. **For most couples, we recommend the joint account method for dual earners.**

While this may sound like a great idea at first, before you get excited thinking about having twice as much money in your bank account, there are some risks associated with this approach. For instance, if you or your spouse have consumer debt or student loans, commingling your finances could make your spouse legally and financially responsible for paying back *your* debt—if payments come from the joint bank account.

This is a shock to most people. It is also why many couples opt to keep their finances separate while still communicating clearly about the family's monetary decisions regularly. However, just having a few conversations isn't enough for some married couples.

One option to help keep your own financial side of the street clean is to create a prenuptial agreement, often referred to as a "prenup." You can list the premarital debt on a prenuptial agreement so that it covers you in the case of a financial incident. Most people are familiar with prenups because they help protect a wealthy person from losing a large amount of money in a divorce. However, that's not the only reason they can be helpful. Even if you keep your accounts separate, you have to be very aware.

If your paychecks go into a joint account—and you start paying out of the joint account to pay off something like student loans—creditors can view that as an accepted obligation to share that debt. The same is true if you ever make credit card payments from a joint account. It implies that both of you are responsible for the debt. If your spouse has $80k in student loans, and they die suddenly, you may be responsible for their debt. With a prenup, this type of financial nightmare could easily be avoided. As always, if this issue of a student loan applies to you, please consult with a qualified attorney to get their opinion on the issue.

As members of the *Family Business*, you should hold monthly financial meetings (just like a business would) to discuss questions such as, "Are we on budget?" "What is left over?" or "What can we cut out that we don't need to spend money on?" These aren't questions you can just ask once. The family budget is one area where you must remain diligent (and sometimes vigilant) about your spending. It is not a category where you can just "set it and forget it." Budgets constantly change. Review these questions at least once a month to make sure your family stays on track.

Having Children (or a Pet) Can Be a Financial Decision

In life, the decision to have children is one of the most rewarding decisions you can ever make (note: many of the same items apply to raising a pet). We have both enjoyed the rewards of parenthood more than any other lifestyle choice decision we have ever made. But like it or not, raising children is a financial decision that will impact you for at least two decades until your child can secure a job or enroll in college, and even then, they may still be partially dependent on you financially.

The reality is that the decision to have kids can slow you down on your journey toward financial freedom. We don't say that flippantly, but like it or not, it is a financial truth. Having children may very likely be part of your *true wealth* goal. True wealth refers to all the things money cannot buy and death cannot take away. There is an emotional component to this type of intangible wealth. If having children is a priority for you, you'll want to start saving and investing early on in your career to help make it easier for you to achieve your goals.

Starting early on the road toward financial freedom means creating budgets and savings plans and adopting good healthy habits. Be thoughtful about the costs that will come up in the years ahead. Daycare, babysitters, diapers, food, playpens, toys, new clothes every few months as the child grows rapidly, tutoring services, piano lessons, gas to and from school, and eventually, potentially financing a car for your teenager will all take a toll on the family budget.

Try to Plan Ahead Financially Before Having Children

The family budget starts with the amount of money you (and your spouse) have after taxes, employer-sponsored retirement contributions, etc. As the size of your family increases, so do your expenses. In dual-earning households, the annual salary will also increase (thanks to the fact that both of you are now working). The biggest expenses for your family will be the 50% portion of your budget devoted to "needs" like housing, food, medical expenses, and childcare. The money left over after these expenses get covered is the amount you get to work with each month. How you choose to spend this money will help determine how quickly you reach millionaire status.

Let's look at some key areas you should consider *before* starting a family.

- **Housing** costs usually increase. Rent payments often graduate to become mortgage payments as the family expands.

- **Food** costs and weekly grocery store visits will increase.

- **Transportation** will become more expensive (a larger SUV is a good example)

- **Utility Payments**: Electricity, Gas, and Water will increase as more people use the utilities in the house.

- **Insurance Payments**: Health, Life, Auto, Home, and Disability will become more of a priority.

- **Medical Expenses and Healthcare**: Above and beyond premiums, you will need to start budgeting for out-of-pocket expenses, deductibles, nutrition, wellness expenses, and dental items.

- **Saving and Investing**: Emergency reserve and short/mid/long-term savings will now be more important with multiple mouths to feed.

Your six-month emergency fund will also need to increase as your monthly expenses rise.

- **Childcare**: Babysitters, daycare, schooling, tutoring, and after-school activities can all add up quickly.

Keep in mind, if you're just starting your financial savings journey, the first year after you get married may not be the best time to have a baby. However, perhaps it is after a few years, as you'll have amassed more assets. Delaying having children can aid your journey toward financial freedom. Once you start having kids, saving 20% of your income becomes more challenging. Just like climbing a mountain, sometimes you encounter snow and have to make camp, returning to your plan later. It's easy to stray from the path and take a rest, but it's much harder to muster the motivation to return to it. Once children enter the equation, unexpected expenses, sleepless nights, and missed workdays begin to creep into your life. Parenthood is an immense responsibility; the needs of children never take a day off, and their illnesses don't consider how many vacation days you have remaining. It might be hard to visualize if you're child-free, but if you want to adhere to your savings plan, you'll likely need to cut back on your wants, not your needs. It's all about balance and compromise. Having children while maintaining financial savvy is entirely possible. Just ensure you find equilibrium. Set a family budget and adhere to it. But remember, it's not solely about staying on budget; it's also about keeping your priorities in order.

Mark recalls that when he got married, his and his wife's monthly mortgage payment was $391. That figure may seem low by today's standards, but for him, it wasn't the mortgage that disrupted his budget. At just 25, he was already driving his dream car, an Audi A6 Quattro. It was a fantastic vehicle— in fact, it was the car in which he took his son home from the hospital. One of the nurses even remarked that most newborns don't get chauffeured home in such a fancy ride. She didn't know that Mark's monthly car payment was

$540—nearly $150 more than his mortgage! Before fatherhood, Mark could afford his car, but once he committed to marriage and children, his financial priorities had to change. As a young father and husband, Mark learned the hard way that his individual budget needed to yield to the family budget. He managed to transform a poor purchase decision into a beneficial one by keeping the car for over ten years. In your journey through family life, you will also face tough decisions.

We suggest saving as much as you can as early as possible so that your early sacrifices will turn into early financial victories to help your family get on the road to financial freedom faster.

Simple Road Recap:

In this chapter, we explained how marriage is like creating a "Family Business," complete with a revised family budget (that will now have to be updated from your personal budget that you created in Chapter 2). We also explained some of the new items that you will need to account for, such as the financial costs of having children and how to think about sharing/splitting bank accounts with your spouse.

CHAPTER 18

Life Insurance - STL CHECKPOINT

Weatherman Phil Connors, played by Bill Murray, finds himself in a precarious predicament in the classic film *Groundhog Day*. He realizes he is stuck in a repetitive time loop, reliving the same day, February 2nd, over and over. One of the worst parts of being trapped in this never-ending cycle is encountering an old, annoying classmate, Ned Ryerson. Ned, an insurance salesman, feigns kindness while attempting to sell Phil life insurance. Day after day, Phil devises clever and creative ways to avoid this conversation about a product he has no interest in purchasing. Finally, in desperation, Phil delivers a roundhouse punch to Ned's nose, clearly conveying his disinterest.

When the average person thinks about life insurance, they might envision pushy insurance salesmen like Ned. Their reaction is usually no different from Phil's—life insurance is a topic that no one wants to discuss. It's a *snooze alert*! But what if we told you that life insurance isn't as boring as you might think? The following might sound like the setup for a novel, but we assure you, it's not. It's a real scenario that could unfold for you and your family due to not purchasing life insurance.

Imagine the following scenario:

> *You are 45 years old, and you've done well for yourself. You have three beautiful children, a spouse who loves you, and your salary is $150,000*

per year. Life is going perfectly, and because things are going so well, your spouse has recently resigned from their job to spend more time with the kids. Life is great until one day, it's not.

You're driving home from the office one night, and there's a six-car pileup. You swerve madly to avoid a collision, but despite digging the soles of your shoes into the brake pedal, you can't stop in time. Your final thoughts are of your family being left to fend for themselves. You don't survive.

Shortly after your accident, the bills start rolling in, and there are no longer any paychecks. Funeral expenses, costly daycare, and wasted months of your spouse hunting for a new job leave your family in dire straits. With 20 years left until retirement, your family is burning through their savings. The adjustment is incredibly difficult financially, psychologically, and emotionally because your family is used to spending $100,000 per year on expenses. A lifestyle of a beautiful home with a significant mortgage, nice vacations, fancy dinners, piano lessons, and dance classes for the kids really adds up. Now, your family is forced to cut back and count their pennies until your spouse can get back on their feet and secure income. Even when they land a job, the family's earning power is never quite what it used to be. Life is much harder in the wake of your devastating accident.

Life insurance, just like car insurance, is there when you need it. You hope that you'll never cash in on your policy. In fact, national averages state that most term life insurance policies never pay out a death benefit. That's a good thing. We hope that everyone reading this book is lucky enough to never need their insurance. No one ever buys a brand-new car, thinking they will total it. Life insurance is no different.

Part of being a responsible spouse or parent is planning ahead for your family's financial destiny. Life insurance is a simple way to protect yourself in case something happens to you or your spouse. The death benefit is the most important aspect of your life insurance plan.

Long story short, you need life insurance to protect you and your budget in case something happens to the primary income earner.

Simple Summary: Insurance is used to Cover Lost Income

Think of your insurance payout as a replacement for your salary. In theory, your need for life insurance should decrease each year as you earn more money and save more for retirement. You want to ensure you have enough money in the death benefit to cover your family's budget for years to come.

When you have a young family and your spouse dies, it can take a year or more before the surviving partner reenters the workforce. You can never predict how the surviving spouse will react to a crisis. You also can't foresee the dynamics of what will transpire within the family in the event of your sudden death. Careers change. Children need care and grief counseling. Life happens.

As a parent or spouse, let's consider this from another perspective. People often resist the idea of spending money on life insurance because it seems like a waste. Let's remove the human element from the equation for a moment. Pretend you are a machine that prints money. Month after month, you produce money that your family uses for their expenses. Everyone in your family expects that machine to keep generating cash, much like an ATM. If suddenly the machine breaks down and stops functioning, the other family members who depend on that breadwinner will face difficulties. You need a backup plan—that's what a life insurance policy provides. In our example above, if a family is counting on the $150,000 salary for the next 20 years, then they'll need at least a $3 million policy to replace that income.

Spoiler alert: most people only need their life insurance policy to insure their estimated future income until retirement.

We recommend insuring yourself for the potential loss of income to cover the paychecks you will miss after your death. In most cases, having enough term life insurance to replace your annual income until retirement is likely all you need. Just because you hope your policy won't pay out doesn't mean it's a wasteful monthly expense. If you pass away, your income is automatically replaced for a fraction of its cost. This single decision could save your family's financial future. Don't procrastinate.

We'll review some basics to give you a better understanding of how life insurance functions. We can't endorse a one-size-fits-all plan suitable for every family, but we can present the key facts and allow you to make an informed decision. Whichever plan you select, having one is crucial. In Mark's twenty-six years as an advisor, he has never had a beneficiary refuse the proceeds of an insurance contract because they disliked the type of policy the deceased had chosen. In other words, obtaining insurance—whether it's a term policy, whole life, or universal—is more critical than waiting to find the perfect plan. The most important thing is to ensure that your policy adequately meets the needs and desires of those you leave behind.

Here's a summary of what we will be covering in the rest of this chapter.

Our Recommendations for Insurance:
- **Term Life Insurance**
- **Disability Insurance**

Here Are Other Popular Options:
- **Whole life**
- **Universal life**

Let's explore some of the most common life insurance policies.

1. Term Life Insurance

Spoiler alert: we strongly suggest that you purchase term life insurance over the other forms.

Think of term life insurance as similar to your auto and home insurance. You pay a premium, and you have coverage for a set "term." When you stop paying, you lose coverage, which ends once that "term" is over, akin to car insurance. The death benefit for term life only pays out if you pass away before the term you purchased expires. Most people will outlive their insurance policy, which is fortunate.

Term life insurance is most commonly bought in periods such as 5, 10, 15, 20, or even 30 years. The advantage of buying a locked-in period is that the rate remains the same every year of the term policy. Term life insurance is suitable for someone looking for relatively inexpensive but very valuable coverage. <u>What's most important is you pick the proper amount and term when you initially purchase it,</u> so you don't have to purchase it again when the cost can be prohibitive (because you're insuring yourself at an older age, which presents more risk for the insurance company).

The prices for buying term life insurance vary among insurance companies, so it's important to shop around to get the best deal. Factors that can affect your rates include:

- Smoker/non-smoker
- Height and weight
- Gender

A physical is usually required before you can purchase a life insurance policy. Most insurance companies will send out their own nurse to perform the physical. Often, they'll take blood and urine samples, and they will likely hook you up to a heart monitor. Some policies may require the applicant to go to a facility for additional testing. The underwriting process helps determine if the person to be insured is insurable and, if so, at what amount and cost. The insurance industry strives to provide the fairest price for a person's risk. One of the reasons it is wise to invest in life insurance when you are younger is that you are typically healthier, so the cost to insure you will be lower than it would be in the future.

2. Whole Life Insurance

Whole life insurance is just as the name implies—it covers you for your "whole life." Unlike term life insurance, whole life is considered a "permanent" policy. Whole life has a death benefit (like term life) and a cash value that earns interest over time. Each time you make a payment (either annually or monthly), a portion goes toward the insurance cost, and a portion goes to the cash value. A whole life policy could cost 5-15 times more than a term policy with the same death benefit. The cash value aspect makes whole life a bit more complex because of fees, interest, taxes, etc., as they accrue and gain interest over time.

One benefit is that whole life could be an avenue for tax deferral for high-net-worth individuals who have exhausted other deferral areas. But for the average individual, whole life is not a significant tax strategy. Whole life is often illustrated with the "cash value," potentially earning enough to cover the cost of insurance for life as the amount you pay into the policy grows and appreciates over time. These claims, of course, are all subject to the ability of the insurance company to pay dividends and maintain solvency, so always make sure to buy from a reputable insurance company. Remember, you could invest this money and pay for a death benefit (through term life insurance) without paying extra fees.

3. Universal Life Insurance

Universal plans are flexible permanent life contracts that allow you to adjust your premium and death benefits. They are very similar to Whole Life; however, these policies differ in the way the cash value is managed. The cash value in a Universal Life contract is based on fixed interest rates based on market performance. By adjusting the premium that is paid into the contract and/or using policy cash to cover your payment due to its flexible nature, the policy could be subject to underfunding. If this were to happen, the insured/owner would pay more into the contract. Since this can be a confusing option for most people, we would not recommend it for the average person.

Disability Insurance

Death isn't the only thing that can stalwart your family's financial aspirations. Disability can also seriously impact your ability to earn income. Some employers don't offer disability insurance, but you can purchase it on the open market. The cost and availability will be based on your occupation and the risk factors involved with your job. We recommend that you work with an insurance agent who is skilled in navigating the ins and outs of disability insurance. Make sure that it covers your specific skill set because you "may" be able to "work," but you want to make sure it covers your current occupation. A surgeon who can no longer operate could technically still be "employed" and work as a greeter at Walmart earning minimum wage, so you want to make sure the plan covers you and the specific skill sets needed to keep your current income level. Remember, disability insurance differs from long-term care or life insurance, so do your due diligence and see what your employer offers. In most cases, up to 60% of your income is insurable in the event of lost income due to death or disability.

Do Your Homework to Decide What's Best for You

Do your homework—don't always go with the cheapest option. Weigh the risks and make sure the plan you select is covering what needs to be covered. Find out what dollar amount you need to be protected. And never fully rely on the insurance agent's advice without doing your homework first. Just like Ned Ryerson, they are salespeople by nature. They earn their salary and steep commissions based on you buying their products. Often, they will try to sell you the most expensive product that earns them the greatest sales commission. Insurance agents can make as much as a 65% commission on a whole-life insurance plan.

The moral of the story is to look hard at these plans, the devils in the details. Life insurance is an investment, even though it is an insurance product. You can get great coverage and invest in the market in other ways—rather than paying for a whole life insurance plan.

A Word of Caution:

We do not recommend canceling any insurance coverage until you have done your homework and have implemented a new policy with full coverage. Since life insurance is based on your health and several other factors, there is no guarantee that coverage will be approved for you. We would hate to see you cancel one policy, hoping to upgrade to a better plan and discover that you are uninsurable. Always do your homework before you commit to a policy.

Our Recommendation

Term life insurance is nice because it can be changed. Rates for term are based on your age. But the caveat for young families is that term life insurance is so cheap in your 20s that it can be very cheap to establish great coverage. If you wait until you are in your 30s (just like waiting to start investing in a Roth IRA or 401(k)), getting the type of death benefit you want can be much more expensive. When you are planning to have a family, you want to get started thinking ahead as soon as possible. If you can, start planning ahead before you have your first child; it will help you to get your finances in order first.

We recommend buying term life insurance and investing the difference between the term premium and the whole-life premium. Often, if this is something you're going to tap into 10-20 years down the line, placing that extra money in something like an S&P 500 index fund will potentially get you a greater ROI over time. Here's an example that illustrates this point.

Example:

$1 million term life policy: $30 per month
Whole life policy with $1 million death benefit: $150 per month

As mentioned in the example above, we would suggest going with the term life policy and investing the $120 per month that you save compared to the whole life policy. This strategy will save you fees and commissions that come standard with a whole life policy.

Term life is the only policy that lets you know exactly what you are signing up for. In most cases, term life insurance is a more appropriate solution.

When it comes to life insurance, take a hard look at your employer plan if they offer it—that may be your least expensive option. If you do participate in a group life insurance benefit plan, you want to make sure it is "portable," so make sure that you don't lose your benefits if you lose your job. Otherwise, you potentially risk losing your benefits if you get terminally ill.

Don't Delay this Decision

If you are considering getting life insurance, don't delay that decision. We understand that it can feel overwhelming at first to think about these long-term financial decisions. However, if you are serious about your family's well-being, commit to purchasing life insurance in the next two weeks.

Mark once had an eager couple come into his office to finalize their life insurance plan. A check was needed to pay the first month's premium and activate the policy. The couple balked at paying it right there in the office because they didn't have their checkbook. After all, it was no big deal—their policy would start in a month. Three weeks later, the husband suffered a heart attack and died. You never know what is going to happen tomorrow. Whether you are 25 or 65, life happens. If you think you will need it—why not get it done today?

Simple Road Recap:

In this chapter, we explored the importance of life insurance. We looked at some of the most popular types of life insurance coverage and explained the concept of insuring your family against lost future income in the event of an untimely death. We recommend purchasing a term life insurance policy and ensuring you have disability coverage for added protection.

CHAPTER 19

Estate Planning Simplified

When you hear the term estate planning, you may think about massive estate sales or scenes from movies where a will is being read, like Wes Anderson's *The Grand Budapest Hotel.* The bickering potential heirs are gathered in a room with expensive antique furniture, sitting on the edge of their seats, waiting for an officer of the court, who looks like Jeff Goldblum, to come and dictate to them who gets what. Most people shrug their shoulders when they hear the term "estate" and think, *I don't have an estate; this doesn't apply to me.* Even if you aren't a millionaire right now, *everyone* reading this book needs to think ahead about how you want your money to be distributed after you die.

Estate planning isn't only for the upper class; it's for anyone who has any amount of wealth. As soon as someone acquires wealth or debt, they should consider estate planning. A will, one of the simplest ways to manage your estate, allows you to designate who gets your money and assets. Even if the sum of your assets is a savings account with just $10,000 in it, that money could be life-changing for a grandchild, elderly parent, or entrepreneurial sibling looking to start a new business.

But estate planning is *especially important* if you have a spouse or children depending on you for income. Just like life insurance, estate planning is something that you hope happens well after retirement age. However, no one is promised tomorrow. The only thing that is promised is that you won't live forever. One day, like it or not, your estate will be divided up and passed out to your loved ones. It's much better to plan ahead and leave behind your wishes for how you want that process to work than letting a judge decide.

Some people don't want to go through the estate planning process because they don't want to spend the money or take the time to put a plan in place. If you decide not to put an estate plan in place, your money could be subject to significant fees in the form of commissions paid to attorneys and probate officers. These fees will come out of your family's pockets, as those funds allow strangers to determine where your money should go.

Will

Wills have been around a long time, and for good reason. You've probably heard the expression, "Where there's a will, there's a way." In the case of modern-day estate planning, where there's a will, there's no pandemonium among your heirs and family members. A will is a legal document that expresses your wishes for how you want your assets divided up among your beneficiaries and how to care for any of your dependents after you die. You may think you don't need a fancy Last Will and Testament, but the reality is that wills are no laughing matter. If you leave a will, you will get to designate an executor to be responsible for carrying out your final wishes. You can leave specific instructions for how you want your children to receive money, who would become their legal guardian (if they are under 18), and which assets you want to be given to your beneficiaries. It makes it all fairly cut and dry, minimizing contentious gray areas that can be the source of a lot of resentment, especially in families.

You can also create a TOD (Transfer on Death), which automatically transfers ownership of things like investment accounts to the person or entity (trust, etc.) you select. IRAs and 401(k)s allow you to designate a beneficiary, so it will automatically go to them in the event of your passing. A will can help you to outline assets that aren't as cut and dry.

Trust

Trust isn't always necessary for every family. For many people, a will is a suitable solution because it tells who the money should go to, and the executor of the will carries out your final wishes. But what if your beneficiaries are minors? Do you want them coming into hundreds of thousands of dollars simultaneously? What if they are eighteen, fresh out of high school? Their dream car is a Ferrari 296 GTB with a sticker price of over $300k. Now that they have your inheritance, they can finally afford it! This may seem like a silly example, but what if you and your spouse pass in a car accident and leave millions of dollars to your 18-year-old? A will hand them the keys to their dream "depreciating asset." However, if you want to control some of your money from the grave—so that your kids don't have access to all of their money all at once, a trust is the way to go. For example, if you have $1 million in your trust, you could ask for it to be disbursed as $50,000 per year for 20 years instead of one lump sum.

When it comes to trusts, there is a buffet of options—Survivor Trusts, Guardianship Trusts, Generation Skipping Trusts, Charitable Remainder Trusts, Charitable Lead trusts, Private Foundations, Rabbi Trusts, Irrevocable Life Insurance Trusts, and Credit Shelter Trusts—just to name a few! However, the good news is that for most people reading this book, there are only two major options: **a revocable trust and an irrevocable trust**. The first option (revocable trust) allows you to make changes. The second option sets your wishes in stone—it is irrevocable—meaning you can't change it without jumping through several legal hoops first. Later in this chapter, we will look at the benefits and drawbacks of both.

Who Are Your Beneficiaries? - STL CHECKPOINT

You may have heard of the term "beneficiary" before. An easy way to remember what this means is to think about who would receive the "benefits" of your estate after you pass. If you're reading this and don't know your beneficiaries, this is a great time to **Stop, Talk** and **Listen**. Often, people don't start thinking about these types of eventualities until after they get married. Sometimes, jobs will ask you to fill out a beneficiary form early on in your career.

One horror story that made national headlines occurred when a husband missed out on his wife's $1 million retirement fund because her beneficiary form listed her sister as her sole beneficiary. She was a teacher and had filled out the form as a young single woman and never updated it. A long, grueling court battle between the husband and his late wife's sister resulted from a simple failure to update her beneficiary.

Most people want their beneficiaries to be their spouses or children. When you have kids, you want to pass on the best pieces of yourself to them. You also want their life to be better than yours. Financially, leaving behind an inheritance is one of the ways that this happens.

Estate planning can be a complex process, depending on how many assets you have. To make things easy, we want to encourage you to focus on four main action steps that will help you to check off estate planning on your to-do list.

The Big Four

In terms of estate planning, you aren't just directing where you want your money to go; you are preparing the Family Business to continue on without its CEO at the helm. When businesses are sold, you better believe the new owner wants the trade secrets that made that business successful. Estate planning is no different. It's important that you communicate your final wishes with your family in writing before you get sick or die. Here are four items to consider:

1. Will

2. Health Care Directive–Who Do You Want to Make Decisions on Your Health?

Advanced medical directives are similar to wills, but in this instance, they direct hospitals and family members regarding your standard of care. These directives are legal protocol documents that assist in making crucial life-or-death decisions on your behalf. They are important if you are incapacitated due to an accident, illness or require advanced medical care. Often, people find themselves wishing their loved one had a medical directive in place when facing situations like a coma, worsening dementia, or end-of-life care. Under these circumstances, the family is often left to make difficult choices because they are unaware of your wishes.

For instance, DNRs (Do Not Resuscitate orders) and DNIs (Do Not Intubate orders) are important instructions that you can leave, providing your family members with some peace of mind, knowing they aren't prolonging your pain unnecessarily. Sudden changes in quality of life, such as terminal illness, a car accident, or other life-changing events, can create painful divides within the family.

Separately, if you have children who are 18 or older, you will want to set up a Medical Power of Attorney for them so that you can participate in making important decisions regarding their care protocol. Otherwise, you risk not being legally involved in their care.

3. Durable Financial Power of Attorney–Who Do You Want to Handle Your Finances When You Can't?

Setting up a financial plan is an important step toward effective estate planning, but what happens if an emergency situation leaves you incapacitated? What if you go into a coma or have a prolonged hospital stay? The bills don't stop arriving in your family's mailbox. As discussed in Chapter 13, the IRS still requires your tax payments. Additionally, someone will need to stay on top of paying the most recent hospital and insurance bills while you are unwell.

A financial power of attorney is a form that allows you to assign someone to manage your finances if you cannot do so yourself. The person assigned can complete necessary financial tasks like paying bills, filing taxes, keeping your business running, or managing your investments or real estate properties on your behalf, acting as you. This arrangement is crucial to ensure that your family maintains their quality of life in your absence.

One important caveat to note is that you'll want to ensure your financial power of attorney is designated as a "durable power of attorney." This designation is critical because it allows your appointed agent to continue acting on your behalf if you become incapacitated. A general power of attorney only operates while you are coherent and mentally capable, automatically expiring upon incapacity or death. In contrast, a durable power of attorney remains in effect upon incapacity but does expire upon death.

You can choose not to grant them durable power of attorney, but it's important to understand that if you go into a coma, suffer from dementia, or have another reason for incapacitation, they won't legally be able to act on your behalf. Durable financial power of attorney removes these barriers.

Don't worry; just because someone holds this power doesn't mean they will use it without your consent. It's akin to when the President of the United States undergoes surgery. Technically, the Vice President is sworn in and assumes the role of acting President. They assume this role temporarily until the incapacitated President recovers and resumes their duties. It's a temporary transition of power, nothing more, nothing less. If your family relies on you to manage their finances, having a backup in place—even if you never need it—is well worth the time and effort to set up. Usually, a doctor or independent third party needs to document your incapacity before this power is activated.

4. Revocable Trust or Irrevocable Trust

A revocable trust allows you to maintain control over your assets until you die or are incapacitated. You can appoint a trustee to manage the trust and execute your wishes after you die. One of the main advantages a revocable trust offers is that it gives you flexibility with how assets are distributed, and it can be changed at any point.

An irrevocable trust allows your assets to be put into the trust, and effectively the trust owns them. The trust is assigned a tax ID number (TIN). Doing this helps get assets out of the estate so that the trust can own them. This is a very helpful strategy for minimizing estate taxes if you have a sizable estate. An irrevocable trust won't be right for everyone because it is very difficult to make changes once you set up an irrevocable trust. Whereas a revocable trust allows you to make amendments and changes yourself, with an irrevocable trust, you will need to get a third party involved and may even need to petition a court to make changes. For this reason, irrevocable trusts have a certain level of finality involved.

One of the benefits of an irrevocable trust is that once you put assets into the trust, they are potentially shielded from personal creditors or lawsuits. Still, while you technically cannot sue a trust, you can sue the trustee, who is responsible for carrying out the terms of the trust. Moving assets into an irrevocable trust also changes how you pay taxes on these assets. The trust pays taxes since you no longer "own" the assets. For this reason, it is important to work with your financial planner and a CPA to make sure the investments within the trust are more tax-favorable when it comes to trust tax laws. An irrevocable trust reports income on Form 1041, the IRS's trust and estate tax return. Even if a trust is a separate taxpayer, it may not have to pay taxes. If it makes distributions to a beneficiary, the trust will take a distribution deduction on its tax return, and the beneficiary will receive an IRS Schedule K-1.

Estate Tax - STL CHECKPOINT

Currently, 12 states have an additional estate tax. If you have a sizable estate, you will want to think about ways to reduce your state estate tax bill.

For high-net-worth individuals (with estates greater than $4 million) who live in a state subject to estate taxes, most would be well served to put some of their assets into an irrevocable trust. We suggest you put assets that can't be touched during your lifetime in an irrevocable trust—such as a lake house or farm you want to remain in the family.

Our Recommendation

In most cases, having a health care directive, durable financial power of attorney, and a will is a great place to start. But you may also want to consider setting up a trust instead of a will if you have children. There are a lot of trusts out there, but we recommend a **revocable living trust for most people**. A revocable trust can help to solve most of the problems of what to do with your money after you die, especially if you have children. The parameters of a revocable trust can be created so that you can spread out how much your children inherit over time. Just like choosing which life insurance policy, it's important not to procrastinate on this decision.

Simple Road Recap:

This chapter discussed the importance of estate planning and how it is a necessary part of your financial journey—even if you only have a modest savings. We also explored some of the biggest estate planning considerations, such as identifying your beneficiaries. We recommend

doing more research about the Big Four in estate planning: health care directive, durable financial power of attorney, a will, and either a revocable or irrevocable trust (if this applies to your situation).

PART 3

Late-In-The-Game

The Last Leg of the Journey: Mark Reaches the Summit

The journey had been long. Months of planning and preparation had gone into our climb. The guides had traversed this terrain countless times, and with each climb, they learned a little bit more about how to make the journey easier. There were late afternoons when I wanted to press on to get up the mountain faster, but I had to rely on the wisdom of our guides, urging us to hold back and stick to the plan. Just hours later, a storm swept through, which would have been disastrous had we not stopped and established our base camp. I was glad that I had the combined wisdom of others who had walked this same path before me.

There were moments early on when I felt like I was just taking tiny baby steps at a snail's pace. But now, looking ahead, I knew that all of those small actions had led me here. This was the payoff—the reward for all of my hard work, persistence, and dedication.

Careful not to go too fast—I slowed down to enjoy the picturesque view, for a fall at this height would obviously not be good. And just like that, I was finally standing on top of the mountain!

As I was enjoying the view, I curiously asked my guide, pointing to another mountain way off ahead of me, which mountain is that? 'That, my friend, is your next climb.'"

As you reach the final stretch of your financial mountain, you are probably in your late forties or fifties. The road to the summit is clear—retirement looms ahead on the horizon. By now, if you aren't already a millionaire—assuming you've followed the advice in this book—you're hopefully close. Every step you take at the end matters. At this height, a fall off the mountain would irreparably damage your financial health. Don't get complacent if you finally reach the top of the mountain and join the million-dollar club. Remember, there's always a higher peak out there, just waiting for you to climb it. If you haven't joined the million-dollar club, or even if you have, now may be a good time to double back on the concepts at the beginning of the book. Oftentimes, people who are "late-in-the-game" have significant salaries, and usually, some prior costs might be in the rearview mirror, like raising children, a mortgage, or other debt. We suggest you take some time and make sure you're maximizing your opportunities based on the topics we've covered up to this point in the book before diving into this next stage of the climb.

CHAPTER 20

Death and Inheritance

At some point, everyone has imagined what it would be like to inherit a great deal of money. It's the ultimate fantasy. It's easy to close your eyes and start salivating over all the ways you could spend money you didn't have to work for. Most Americans secretly hope they will inherit a million dollars from Great Aunt Gertrude (whom they never even knew existed), believing that, just like Forrest Gump, their lives will change dramatically overnight. However, for the majority of people who will endure the pain and grief of losing loved ones, an inheritance can be summed up in just four little words:

1. Don't
2. Count
3. On
4. It

Many people naively assume a hidden pot of gold is waiting for them at the end of the rainbow. They hold out, fingers crossed, hoping this windfall will solve all their financial problems.

How Much is Actually Left?

While you may dream of running off to buy beachfront property on some exotic island with your loved one's inheritance, the average inheritance in the

US might disappoint you. Experts suggest that the average inheritance is between just $45,000 and $90,000. Keep in mind this is just an average. Some inheritances will be much larger, and others will be much smaller. No matter the size of the inheritance you receive, the important thing to focus on is how you invest it. Saving it may not be as fun as buying a new Tesla S, but you'll be glad you invested the money wisely in a few years.

Some people get so wrapped up in the idea of mom and dad's money swooping in to save them from their financial hardships that they are in for a very rude awakening when their parents pass. Inheritance is usually a false hope. It's the mirage at the end of a financial desert.

Often, people will use the prospect of a large inheritance as an excuse to make poor financial decisions. Instead of wisely investing their money when they are young and practicing delayed gratification, they shrug their shoulders and assume that one day they'll get lucky with a big check from their parent's life savings. Remember, just because your parents have money today doesn't mean there will be money left over tomorrow.

Predicting how long your parents' money will last is always a moving target. No one can predict future health problems or whether a parent will need extra care or assisted living. Nursing homes and retirement communities can be very expensive. Unless you are the executor of your parents' estate, you may not have a clear financial picture of what's really in their portfolio. Time and time again, children don't have a good gauge of their parents' expenses in retirement. The only real guarantee is that making assumptions about inheritance is a clear-cut recipe for disappointment.

Remember, assets aren't the only thing you can inherit—*you can also inherit your parents' debt.* If your parents die owing back taxes, you inherit that old tax bill and become responsible for paying it out of your parents' estate. Other secured debts will also need to be paid back, which can greatly cut into how much is left over for your inheritance.

Another factor you'll want to consider is that every family situation is unique. Money has a way of creating divides and false illusions, especially within families. There is no greater instance of this than with an inheritance. Sometimes, parents want to divide their estate unevenly, meaning some children will get more than others. Often, there is a lack of communication between parents and their children about realistic numbers for their retirement savings and other assets. Parents may be ashamed that they can't live up to the societal expectation of leaving behind a sizable fortune for their children, so they lead them to believe that there is more money in the estate than there really is. To sum it up, some people would actually rather die than have an honest and frank discussion with their children about their finances.

For that reason, we encourage you to think about inheritance, like winning the lottery. It would be incredible if it happened, *but don't count on it.* If you are lucky enough to receive an inheritance, invest it wisely. Be especially careful if you inherit a lump sum all at once. Since that is often what happens, let's discuss that for a moment.

Lump Sums

Studies have shown a depressing fact about how people behave with lump sums. When people get a lump sum of "free money," whether it is an inheritance or lottery winnings, it is usually gone in just a couple of years. Two short years of fun and frivolous spending may sound like the time of your life—and it may be—but eventually, your fun will come to an abrupt end.

The reality about lump sums is that they are one of the rare moments where you get "free money." If you put that money to work for you in your late 40s or early 50s—by the time you retire, it could really help fast track your road toward financial freedom. For this reason, we recommend that you don't use lump sums to change your "lifestyle." Sure, they are nice to have, but there is an old saying, "Money you didn't work for spends twice as quickly." If you get a sizable inheritance, allowing you to retire earlier than you thought, great. But stay within your budget, and don't upgrade your lifestyle overnight.

How to Invest an Inheritance - STL CHECKPOINT

After receiving an inheritance, the first thing you will want to do is revisit your current budget and financial summary. By this point in the book, we probably sound like a broken record—but revisiting your budget is one of the most prudent financial decisions you can make regularly. Think of it like glancing down at the speedometer while driving on the highway. You don't need to know exactly how fast you are going at every moment, but it is important to periodically check in to see where you are at. Sometimes, a slower driver or other obstacle will slow you down. If you don't periodically check in, you might not realize how fast or how slow you are going toward your destination. The same is true with your budget.

Follow the guide we set at the beginning of the book: If you have credit card debt or other forms of high-interest debt, pay them off first. Prioritize these high-interest debts and pay them off as soon as possible. If you don't have "bad debt," then you may want to invest your inheritance into a college fund for your children if you haven't done so already. After you've invested in these two areas, the next thing you need to do is pause and reflect on what's really important in the years ahead.

NOTE: The main point we want to make is that if you receive an inheritance, large tax refund, or any large amount of unexpected money, treat it just like you would a workplace bonus and stick to your original game plan. You don't need to come up with a whole new plan.

Look Into Unclaimed Property

The average life expectancy is around 75. In seven decades, people can acquire numerous assets. Many times, people have assets they forget about (or move), and money meant for them doesn't make it to the right people. Sometimes, this money is right underneath your nose, but it gets lost in the shuffle. In some cases, your parents and deceased loved ones will have assets and unclaimed property that you may not have known about, so it is always important to double-check if this is the case.

Today, many states have websites where you can look up any unclaimed assets. For example, the National Association of State Treasurers (MissingMoney.com) has a section for each state that allows you to search for any unclaimed property. Don't forget, if you've moved throughout your lifetime, you should look up each state where you've lived. Things such as bank accounts, insurance proceeds, and check refunds that don't get 'claimed' by the recipient must be turned over by the company issuing the check to the division at the state office that handles Unclaimed Property.

Sometimes, this can translate to "found money," which is essentially "free." You can search by name or address. You will need to have documentation that you are the person trying to claim the property or that you're the authorized person to receive it from someone deceased. There is usually a verification process where they must validate your credentials before sending you the funds.

Don't Make Major Financial Decisions When You Are Emotional

Whatever you decide to do with your inheritance, make sure that you let some time pass before making any major financial decisions. Don't make big decisions that will affect you for years into the future when you are grieving or really excited (about new money). Don't make the mistake many people make when they inherit new money: thinking their financial IQ increased with a nice infusion of cash. Make sure that you are always diligent when seeking financial advice. Sometimes, financial advisors will tell clients what they want to hear just to get their business, which isn't always in their clients' best interest. Prioritize working with someone who has your best interest at heart and listen to their wisdom.

Simple Road Recap:

This chapter discussed inheritance and how to plan for a large cash windfall. Many people overestimate how much inheritance they will receive. Often, this leads them to make poor financial decisions, hoping that one day they will "get caught up" once they receive a large inheritance. Remember, if you get extra money, stick to the 50/20/30 plan and prioritize your investments and savings over your wanted items.

CHAPTER 21

Social Security

The year was 1935. The lingering tragedy of "Black Thursday" and the start of the Great Depression were solidly in the rearview mirror. Now, stuck in the middle of the Great Depression, the eye of the storm, Americans looked for a way out. President Roosevelt was halfway through his first term in office when he unveiled the latest in his New Deal reform initiatives, an office known as the *Social Security Administration*.

He was attempting to help recover the savings and pensions that hard-working Americans had seen swallowed up by the devastating stock market crash six years earlier. At that time, Social Security was to be collected at age 65. Today, we can read that number with a straight face. It's only a couple of years off from our current retirement age. But back then, the average life expectancy was... *are you sitting down?* Good.

In 1935, if you were a shrewd gambler, you'd place your bets on the average life expectancy being just *58 for men and 62 for women*. Not many people lived long enough to see the benefits of FDR's latest initiative.

Contrast that with today's experience of Social Security, and it makes for quite the dichotomy. To us today, this would be the equivalent of saying that you can't collect Social Security until 79 (*adjusted for life expectancy*).

Social Security was one of the original retirement accounts, and it has been a solid program for decades. The goal of this book, however, is to help you plan your retirement so that you don't have to depend on Social Security to retire. It should be viewed as a nice monthly bonus, not a full retirement plan.

For the majority of people reading this book, Social Security checks will be between $1,600-$4,500 per month, on average. This number is calculated by taking your 35 highest-grossing salary years. Therefore, yours will be a little different from your spouse's, so planning ahead for when you want to start withdrawing Social Security is critical to a holistic retirement strategy. Since it is a moving target, let's look at some of the ways to maximize your Social Security benefits.

Deciding When to Start Collecting Social Security Benefits - STL CHECKPOINT

While it can be tempting to delay thinking strategically about how you want to take advantage of this program, Social Security money comes at a crucial time in your life—*retirement*. If you don't think through your family's needs beforehand, it can be a major pitfall and cause you to topple down the financial mountain. By the time you are in your sixties, any financial setback can be disastrous, making it virtually impossible to gather the necessary strength to climb back up the mountain. Once you hit retirement, time is no longer on your side, which means long-term growth can't work its magic quite the same. This is why it is so important that you make sure you are diligent about understanding your financial situation and how your Social Security benefits can help you and your family.

As you think about Social Security, it is important to remember that this program was *never* meant to be the *only* source of income for people when they retire. Social Security was designed to replace a small percentage of a worker's pre-retirement income based on their lifetime earnings. How you manage your retirement income is an art form. The number one absolute truth about Social Security is that there is no one-size-fits-all. The ins and outs of Social Security are a little different for everybody, depending on your working situation. As such, there are a lot of nuances to discuss and some strange rules, numbers, and ages to keep in mind.

Remember, this program is intended for *everyone*, so the following contingency scenarios, age restrictions, and dollar amounts have to factor in every type of contingency and situation for all workers in America. This is why it can look so radically different for different people. The only thing that applies to everyone is that everyone pays into Social Security by being taxed on their first $168,600 per year (as of 2024). If you maxed out your Social Security every year of your working years, your Social Security income will be the same as someone ultra-wealthy like Warren Buffett because everyone is capped at the same level, no matter how much you make above the cap.

What if You Retire Before 67?

Warning: the following sections will throw a lot of numbers, ages, and percentages at you. Don't worry; this is an important step to learning to speak the language of financial literacy. Social Security requirements and stipulations have a lot of "fine print," but knowing the intricacies of the program can help you to collect tens of thousands of dollars more in retirement. It can be the difference between struggling and thriving in your golden years.

As of 2024, the government defines the full retirement age as 67 years old (for people born in or after 1960). That's the age you can start receiving "full retirement" benefits through Social Security payments. The date you retire and when you decide to start taking benefits don't have to be the same, and you don't need to stop working just because you reach full retirement age. You can start drawing Social Security benefits at age 62, but you will receive less benefits. On the other hand, each year you wait to collect past your full retirement age, Social Security will increase benefits until you reach the age of 70—that's the longest the government will let you wait before collecting. If you can afford to wait to collect until your 70th birthday, your Social Security benefits will be worth 8% more every year that you wait (until the cutoff age of 70) than at the full retirement age of 67. But there are some subtle nuances you need to keep in mind before making this important financial decision.

What if I Choose to Work While Drawing Social Security?

Just because the retirement age is set at 67 doesn't mean you must retire. Many people work well into their twilight years. The good news is that if a person works *after* their full retirement age, Social Security will not deduct or penalize you for making too much money in retirement. However, if you start collecting benefits *before* you reach full retirement age and are still working, you can incur penalties for earning too much while collecting Social Security. As of 2024, the threshold for income is $22,320. If you draw Social Security benefits and earn over that limit, you will accrue penalties for earning too much money. And if you earn too much, Social Security will deduct $1 in benefits for every $2 in earnings above the limit. If you have earnings above the threshold in the year you reach your full retirement age (67), Social Security will reduce your benefit by $1 for every $3 you earn over $59,520 (as of 2024). This reduction will be in effect until the month you reach your full retirement age on your 67th birthday. **Remember, you can also start and stop Social Security benefits—so you aren't penalized with new income. Also, what your spouse does won't affect you and your Social Security benefits.**

What Happens if My Spouse Dies?

Survivor benefits are a special aspect of the Social Security program that allows surviving spouses to collect at 60, but there are many exceptions and contingencies. The majority of surviving spouses before age 60 will only receive a paltry (one-time) $255 death benefit. That small check could even be subject to additional taxes.

If your spouse dies and you remarry—you are legally allowed to pick and choose which spouse's Social Security plan you want to collect from. Most people (or at least those who enjoy free money) select the spouse with the most Social Security benefits. (Remember when we said there would be some strange numbers and ages involved in this chapter? Get ready.)

An ex-spouse may qualify for benefits on the former spouse's earnings as long as they had been married for ten years, been divorced from the earner for at least two years if not already collecting benefits, at least 62 years old, unmarried, and their own benefits are not equal or higher. In some cases, if the surviving spouse has a qualifying disability, they can begin collecting at age 50. In even rarer cases, a surviving spouse can collect benefits at any age, so long as they care for the earner's child (who is younger than 16 or has a qualifying disability and is entitled to Social Security on your earnings record)—got all that? Hopefully, this never applies to you, and you don't have to go through the pain of losing a spouse. But if this happens, just remember that you can get help from Social Security to help compensate for your family's lost income and financial hardships.

But benefits aren't just limited to spouses, either. Your surviving children can receive benefits, too, with a couple of exceptions. They must be unmarried and younger than 18. Or they must be between 18 and 19 years old and enrolled full-time in school. If they are 18 or older and have a qualifying disability that started before age 22, they can also receive benefits. Again, we hope this is never something you and your family must endure, but it is nice to know that your children can receive benefits.

Mark had a client who lost her husband to cancer about nine years ago. She and her husband had been married for over 20 years, and he passed away at 53. Thinking she might marry again, she called Mark to ask if there were any financial impacts she should consider.

Mark advised her to think about her Social Security survivor benefits. She was 59 years old, just five months short of turning 60. He counseled her to wait until after her sixtieth birthday to remarry so that she could tap into her former husband's survivor benefits. If she had remarried at 59, she would have forfeited the benefits of her deceased husband. This is why the nuances of the program matter and why it is so important to talk to a qualified financial advisor who can provide you with a holistic overview of where your finances stand before retirement.

Simple Road Recap:

In this chapter, we discussed the high-level ins and outs of Social Security benefits. We recommended considering this money as a supplement, not an actual retirement plan. This is a major STL CHECKPOINT because you must ensure you are maximizing your Social Security benefits in retirement. There are some finer points to understanding this government program, such as when you should retire and start drawing Social Security benefits. We also cover more nuanced topics, like what happens if you've lost a spouse, been divorced, or choose to work while taking Social Security.

CHAPTER 22

A Simple Way to Teach Your Children Financial Literacy

Wouldn't it be nice if there was a simple way to talk to your children about money? It can be difficult for parents to try to explain to their children what it is like to live and work in the "real world." We all know talking about money can be a touchy subject. There are so many excuses for why families don't discuss financial matters gathered around the dinner table. But what if we told you that skipping this conversation could be one of the biggest financial mistakes you'll ever make in your life?

Financial literacy is a skill that can be passed down generationally. It is also a skill set that most adults in today's fast-paced world don't truly understand well enough. As parents, whether you realize it or not, your children strive to emulate you. Even if you choose not to talk openly with your children about money, they still watch everything you do and learn by observing. Subconsciously, they will begin to internalize a story about what money means and how it can be used. If you want to be in control of that story, having a conversation with your child about money provides a safe atmosphere to help guide them to financial success. Parents who teach their children strong financial habits instill a sense of confidence, security, and curiosity about money. Healthy financial habits can be taught at a young age, starting with something as simple as a piggy bank or playing the board game *Monopoly*. It doesn't need to be awkward, complicated, or stress-inducing.

In Mark's experience, most families don't have a financial game plan to communicate with their children about money. Most adults in the U.S. today don't have a strong enough knowledge of the financial system to explain it to their children. We know that talking about finances isn't the easiest topic to explain, which is one of the reasons we wrote this book. Steve likens this conversation to what it was like trying to teach his fifteen-year-old daughter how to drive for the first time.

Despite having driven for decades, he found this conversation difficult. The problem wasn't Steve's knowledge. He knew how to drive. But this conversation was tough because he had no experience teaching *someone else* how to drive. Money management is no different. It requires you to get crystal clear on understanding your own behaviors and reasoning before you can pass on that wisdom to your child.

This is why financial experts struggle to relay their complex financial knowledge and information to everyday people. This is also why your parents may have needed help teaching you about money. Think of financial literacy and illiteracy as two genes—which gene do you want your children to inherit from you?

In this chapter, we want to empower you by providing a simple, three-step framework that you can share with your children to give them a basic understanding of how financial literacy works. The concepts we will share with you are simple enough that you should be able to share them with your children, regardless of age.

Budget, Savings, and Investing

To make this concept as simple as possible, we've narrowed it down to just three easy steps that should be easy for your children to remember. This chapter should feel like a refresher on some of the major points we've already made throughout this book. If you don't have kids or feel you have a good grasp on the big picture, feel free to skip ahead.

Step 1. Budgeting

If you have read this far, then you know budgeting is the bedrock of a solid financial foundation. If you don't have a budget, you will not have a target, and you won't be able to hit your financial goals. It's like playing darts with a blindfold on; it doesn't make much sense not to look at your target. Make sure that you explain to your children that budgets can change on a month-to-month basis. Every time they get a new monthly payment, they will need to update their budget.

Here is a recap of what we would suggest:

- Stick to the 50/20/30 plan: 50% of your income would go to your "needs," 20% to your savings, and 30% to your "wants." Remember to pay yourself first by saving 20% before you start spending on things in your "wants" category. Always stick to the 50/20/30 plan to fast-track your climb up the mountain.
- Make sure to be mindful to base the budget on take-home pay vs. pre-tax salary.

Step 2. Saving

Teach your children that they aren't just saving for next week, next month, or even next year. A portion of every paycheck they get should be earmarked toward funding their retirement. Don't make the mistake countless parents make and think it might be "too early" to talk about retirement savings. Saving for retirement and funding Bucket 3 needs to become a priority as soon as they enter the workforce. An easy way to get them interested in this "grown-up conversation" is to entice them by explaining how they can get "free money" from stock market returns and a potential match at work by contributing to their company-sponsored retirement plans.

MARK SCHLIPMAN & STEVE SHORT

Give them an overview of the Three Bucket System we covered in chapters 4-6.

Step 3. Investing

Investing is one of the most under-discussed financial topics in the educational system. Unless your son or daughter is studying finance or economics at the university level, they will likely not be well-equipped with a basic understanding of how the financial markets work. Teaching children about the wealth-eating force of inflation is important so they understand the natural rise in the cost of living.

- Investing allows you to outpace the rising costs associated with inflation by potentially earning a greater return in the stock market. The longer your money is invested in the market, the more money you can potentially earn.
- Bucket 1 is filled with low-risk investments, Bucket 2 is medium risk, and Bucket 3 is where you can select higher-risk investments.
- We suggest investing in something like an S&P 500 Index mutual fund or ETF.
- It's important to teach children that there is never really a good strategy for "timing the market," the important thing is to invest and leave your Bucket 3 money in the market as long as you can to maximize your potential return on investment.
- Getting started is the hardest part of investing. We suggest helping your child open a brokerage account as soon as they turn 18.

Financial Literacy Can Equal Financial Freedom if You Take Action

One point that we encourage you to really drive home with your kids is the fact that it's not so much about your salary—it's about how you use it. This is so understated in our society. Why? Well, frankly, it's because parents don't educate their children about money. But we live in a society that has an inflated sense of how much money people make. Young people also lack perspective about time, so they rarely prioritize investing their money starting at 18 or in their early 20s. Investing in your 20s could potentially make you a millionaire in your 40s. It's that simple and yet incredibly powerful. Teaching kids to recognize these simple but profound financial truths early will set them up for a lifetime of financial success.

If you don't want your adult children swimming in credit card debt, missing mortgage payments, and constantly asking you for money, start by teaching them financial literacy and best practices at a young age, **especially when they get their first full-time job**. Having this discussion can change your child's life. And not just their lives but also the lives of their entire family for generations to come. Will you pass along prudent financial wisdom? Or will you perpetuate the hands-off approach and let your children fend for themselves financially, just hoping for the best?

Simple Road Recap:

This chapter explored the importance of talking to your children about finances to help them get on the simple road to financial freedom as early as possible, but for sure when they enter the workforce full-time. We gave three major talking points to help guide this discussion.

Number 1: Teach them about creating a budget.

Number 2: Explain to them the importance of savings and the 50/20/30 plan.

Number 3: You will want to encourage them to start investing as soon as they enter the workforce to help them climb the mountain.

CHAPTER 23

Divorce - STL CHECKPOINT

Avoid Common Mistakes During the Divorce

Once you decide to file, couples commonly make several mistakes when going through a divorce. While it may seem odd to have to protect yourself from someone who was your partner in building a family, it is always wise to go into a divorce with open eyes.

1. **Waiting to obtain professional advice**

   One of the first things you will want to do is obtain professional advice. Getting a reputable divorce attorney, a wealth planner, and a divorce counselor are three professionals you should consider hiring right off the bat to help advocate for your financial needs in the divorce.

2. **Failing to educate yourself on the impacts of divorce**

   Many people leave the big decisions up to the lawyers, and they don't take a proactive role in educating themselves on their rights and identifying their long-term needs. Granted, this can be a very taxing process. It is never a fun situation to be in, but it is much better to be prepared for what's ahead. Don't neglect your needs by failing to plan.

3. Refusing to communicate

Divorce can be an unpleasant experience for both spouses. While your partner may be the last person you want to talk to, unfortunately, it is probably a good idea to communicate clearly and effectively. Not communicating may make it more difficult to advocate for your needs during the divorce proceedings. Failing to do so could potentially have unintended consequences. In some situations, less communication is more; defer to your attorney's advice.

4. Forgetting to budget for two households

First off, making sure you have an accurate budget is critical. If you were struggling financially while together, the challenge often intensifies after divorce when you have two households to manage and support. Expenses multiply, encompassing everything from transportation to managing time with children and accommodating new romantic partners, creating a domino effect. Many individuals who are eager to escape the marriage just want the divorce negotiations behind them. Sometimes, they are willing to accept disadvantageous compromises just to expedite the process. However, this is not the time for short-sightedness. The decisions you make with your ex during this process will impact you—and potentially your children—for decades to come.

Too often, people hurry through divorce proceedings without considering the long-term implications of their decisions. It's far easier to address significant financial matters *during the divorce* than *after* everything is finalized. Consider future expenses: who will pay for your daughter's wedding in 18 years or shoulder the costs of college, orthodontic work, dance lessons, or private school tuition? While these considerations may seem far off, establishing a written plan now could save tens of thousands of dollars in the future. Many couples postpone these significant decisions. Relationships can deteriorate, parties may remarry, and your future spouse might end up bearing financial responsibilities that your ex should have assumed as part of a fair divorce settlement.

5. **Assuming a 50/50 division is equitable**

Some couples find themselves "too broke" to afford a divorce, while others are "too rich" to consider it. The division of assets in a divorce, dependent on the state laws governing the process, can be more intricate than a straightforward 50/50 split. Don't expect absolute fairness; there's no unequivocal rule ensuring you or your spouse will receive exactly half of the estate. Various factors, including tax implications and other subtleties, complicate the matter beyond merely dividing all assets down the middle.

For a glimpse into the financial implications of divorce, consider the expenses involved in maintaining a second household; that's essentially what you're undertaking. Legal fees, which are indispensable, can run into tens of thousands of dollars. Counseling, though potentially invaluable, is also costly. Moreover, reentering the dating scene is another significant expenditure. From a financial perspective, divorce is seldom the best option unless it's absolutely necessary.

6. **Agreeing too quickly to a proposed financial arrangement**

Divorce is another time when you will have to take the time and energy to go through your budget again. In many situations, Mark has seen female partners advocate for keeping the family home because of all the memories attached to it. What you want to remember is that the home often comes with debt. Time after time, Mark has to remind couples that the house is a potential liability now due to a lack of income sources. Don't just agree to a proposed financial arrangement because it makes sense at the moment. Think about the big picture in terms of assets. Ask yourself: *What will be most fruitful in the next decade or two?* Don't just settle to make it easier on yourself or your ex-spouse.

7. **Don't overlook "future money"—retirement money and insurance accounts**

One major area that is often overlooked is "future money" in the form of retirement accounts and life insurance policies. One common misconception is that retirement accounts are off-limits to being split up because they have an individual owner. Retirement accounts are considered marital assets and can be split up in the divorce. Sometimes, a settlement may include splitting the assets in a retirement account. One helpful form is a Qualified Domestication Relations Order QDRO, a nontaxable event for both parties. It allows the splitting of a retirement account (per the divorce agreement), which will split the assets to the other spouse. Once the money is moved over, then all the rules of the retirement money are the same as an individual account.

If you are counting on your ex-spouse for monthly payments, you also need to ensure that your ex-spouse has a life insurance policy that would cover you financially in the event of their death. If they have a legal obligation to pay you, they will often also be required by law to have a life insurance policy to cover that potential lost income.

We would suggest you make sure your former spouse is covered by a disability policy where the terms would extend payments to you, as the former spouse, relying on this income. This would need to be written within the divorce agreement.

8. **Putting off the conversation about future financial responsibility**

   Couples undergoing divorce often strive to ease the process for themselves, sometimes inflicting maximum discomfort on the other party. It's crucial during a divorce to delineate key future financial responsibilities. Determining who will handle specific expenses during the separation is far preferable to a contentious and costly dispute years later, should you face an unforeseen bill because you avoided difficult discussions during the proceedings.

   Many individuals overlook crucial financial discussions such as the distribution of assets upon death, responsibility for children's college fees, and the source of those funds. These questions might not have straightforward answers, emphasizing the importance of addressing these issues with your ex-spouse and your team of professionals.

   Consider property implications: if you share a mortgaged home, who continues paying the mortgage, and is the departing spouse entitled to proceeds from a future sale? Some separating couples may need an appraiser to determine the home's value at the time of marriage, ensuring a fair division of any appreciation since then.

   If a business is involved, does your ex-spouse have any outstanding financial claims, ownership shares, or entitlements upon selling the business?

   Additionally, consider shared debts. For example, will you be obligated to continue contributing to your ex-spouse's student loans?

   These complexities underscore the importance of meticulous financial planning during divorce proceedings.

If your head is swimming just from reading all these questions, that's okay. This overview is meant to illustrate what it's like to navigate a divorce from a financial standpoint. Even amicable divorces can be brutal due to the multitude of components that must be considered. Delaying or avoiding these crucial conversations is not a strategy for success. In fact, doing so could result in the most expensive financial mistake of your life, sending you tumbling head over heels down a fiscal precipice. The stakes are indeed that high. Knowing precisely what you owe and the deadlines for each payment is essential to honor your commitments and maintain a clear understanding of your financial standing once the divorce concludes.

After the Divorce–Getting Remarried

In the "Family Budget" chapter, we discussed the significance of a prenuptial agreement in certain situations, such as shielding yourself from a partner's substantial debt. While it may not be the most romantic gesture, our role is not to serve as therapists or dating coaches. From a financial perspective, a prenup can safeguard both parties from unintended long-term economic repercussions, particularly in the context of a second marriage following a divorce.

The dynamics are more intricate in a second marriage. Generally, arranging a prenup for your second marriage is more complex than for your first. As previously mentioned, a prenup enables you to defend your assets and yourself, and typically, individuals possess more assets by the time they remarry. A prenup is a highly cost-effective method to establish transparent expectations and avert or address fiscal issues that, if neglected, could potentially culminate in another divorce in the future. This contract can delineate the specifics of your financial arrangements and assign responsibility for various expenses, all documented in writing before you declare, "I do." Addressing these financial considerations before you tie the knot is crucial, allowing you to relax and concentrate on forging a new life with your partner.

Simple Road Recap:

In this chapter, we explored the financial impacts of getting a divorce, which can become a "fall-off-the-mountain" moment. We shared some things you can do to protect yourself financially *before, during,* and *after* a divorce. Some of the main points we highlighted are hiring professionals, communicating with your spouse before filing, and advocating for yourself during the divorce. We also recommend setting up a game plan for all ongoing future expenses split between you and your spouse (like children's needs) after the divorce is finalized.

CHAPTER 24

Reaching The Summit

Congratulations on completing this book from cover to cover! Climbing a mountain requires significant sacrifice, determination, and inner resilience to endure the ascent. As we've reiterated throughout, life's trade-off decisions compel you to discern what truly matters to you. Each choice you make propels you either one step closer to or further from your aspirations, dreams, and objectives. By dedicating yourself to studying and understanding these financial concepts, you are leagues ahead of where you started when you first opened this book. We recognize that formulating a strategy to reach the summit is an immense task, but we hope you've discovered just how straightforward it can be to follow the steps outlined in this book to achieve your financial freedom.

For many among you, the concepts introduced here may be entirely fresh. We've tried to offer a bird's-eye view of fundamental principles, financial pitfalls, and transformative money habits that have guided hundreds of Mark's clients on their journeys to becoming millionaires. We've assisted you in establishing a robust financial foundation based on enduring principles that will benefit you for many years to come. While these concepts might feel novel now, we trust that, over time, they will become deeply ingrained money management habits you deploy daily.

Rather than hastily spending your paychecks, we encourage you to formulate a budget and adhere to our 50/20/30 rule. While your peers may frequently upgrade their cars, we hope you choose to maximize your retirement contributions, thereby investing in your future. (This approach will endure far longer and potentially be exponentially more valuable in a decade than a brand-new, flashy Mercedes.) Exercising delayed gratification and valuing incremental, steady steps in wealth accumulation will expedite your journey to the summit. The higher you ascend, the more adept you'll become at identifying money-saving measures, much as seasoned climbers discern new pathways that ease their climb. Ensure you remain vigilant during our **STL CHECKPOINTS** to avoid any regressions down the mountain at pivotal stages of your ascent.

The tips and secrets we've taught you in this book may seem like small victories, but in the grand scheme of things, these are huge milestone moments for you. Page by page, chapter by chapter, by reading this book, **you have already walked every single step of the road toward financial freedom.** Sure, you have some work to do as soon as you put this book down. But you have a serious advantage that most Americans don't—you are now equipped with a game plan and a financial roadmap that will guide you mile after mile on your climb to your first million dollars.

While we can't promise that you'll be as lucky as Forrest Gump and get rich off of an investment in the next up-and-coming "fruit company," we can assure you that after reading this book, you have a preview of coming attractions for what lies ahead for you on your road to financial freedom. Take a second to let that feeling of accomplishment soak in. You are now more well-versed in handling your finances than a vast majority of adults! As the introduction promised, we want you to walk away armed with the knowledge and confidence to know how to make it to the top of the mountain.

Welcome to the summit!

After reaching the million-dollar mark in your portfolio, you technically become a "millionaire." Often, this milestone gives people a significant boost in financial confidence. While you might feel tempted to kick back and relax after achieving your goal, we encourage you to maintain the momentum. Having experienced the rewards of delayed gratification and commitment to a sustainable, achievable goal, consider setting your sights on your next challenge. Some of you might wish to channel new funds into a new business venture, while others may dream of traveling the world with their children while working remotely. However, for most readers of this book, we're hopeful the next climb will be getting your next million.

Regardless of your objective, the skills and habits that facilitated your first million will serve as your compass, guiding you to the summit of your next venture. Financial experts often hold varying opinions, but there's near-unanimous agreement on one aspect: earning your second million is considerably easier than earning your first. This ease is due not only to potentially snowballing returns and larger investment sums but also to the solid, consistent habits that underpin the achievement of any goal. This principle is the magic behind this book's simplicity, and we're thrilled for you to put these strategies to the test.

What about those who have finished the book and find themselves facing a daunting journey ahead? Whether you're still living paycheck to paycheck, haven't started investing, or haven't even opened a brokerage account, we believe in you wholeheartedly. The journey can indeed be a simple step-by-step process. Begin with reshaping your mindset, devise a budget, and initiate your savings for retirement and investment ventures. The formula is surprisingly straightforward. Its magic unfolds when you perform these simple tasks repeatedly and consistently. Just as with exercising, the results don't show after only a few sessions at the gym; it takes time.

Knowing that this process can help you, we want to preemptively congratulate you on reaching the mountain's peak. Hopefully, sooner or later, you'll potentially be the one sharing anecdotes over dinner about acquiring your first million instead of listening to a financial professional recount their experiences.

And when your friends ask you how you did it, we hope you will look them in the eye with a kind and gentle smile and say, "It was actually really simple."

THANK YOU FOR READING OUR BOOK!

As a token of our appreciation, we would like to offer you a free gift we are confident will be helpful on your journey toward financial freedom.

Please visit: www.simpleroadbook.com/gift

Or

Simply Scan the QR Code Here:

company or from your financial professional. The prospectus should be read carefully before investing or sending money.

An investment in a Money Market Fund is neither insured nor guaranteed by the Federal Deposit Insurance Corporation or any other government agency. Although the fund seeks to preserve your $1.00 per share, it is possible to lose money in the fund.

Bank certificate of deposits are insured by an agency of the Federal government and offer a fixed rate of return, whereas both the principal and yield of investment securities will fluctuate with changes in market conditions. For Brokered CDs, The Annual Percentage Yield (APY) represents the interest earned through the maturity date. Rates are simple interest calculations over a 365-day basis. Interest cannot remain on deposit. Early redemptions are subject to prevailing market conditions that could result in a loss of principal. The Broker/Dealer does not guarantee the term of the CD. There are some unique differences between traditional bank CDs and brokered deposits:

- *CDs purchased directly from the bank may face an interest penalty if redeemed prior to maturity.*
- *Brokered CDs cannot be redeemed back to the institution prior to maturity.*
- *Early redemption or liquidation prior to maturity may be an amount less than the original price.*

Distributions from traditional IRAs and employer-sponsored retirement plans are taxed as ordinary income and, if taken prior to reaching age 59½, may be subject to an additional 10% IRS tax penalty. A Roth retirement account offers tax-free withdrawals on taxable contributions. To qualify for the tax-free and penalty-free withdrawal of earnings, a Roth account must be in place for at least five tax years, and the distribution must take place after age 59½, or due to death or disability. Depending on state law, Roth account distributions may be subject to state taxes.

A diversified portfolio does not assure a profit or protect against loss in a declining market.

Dollar-cost averaging will not guarantee a profit or protect you from loss, but may reduce your average cost per share in a fluctuating market.

Cryptocurrencies, Digital Assets, and other Blockchain-related technology (such as Bitcoin, Ethereum, NFTs and others) are not securities, not regulated, and not approved products offered by Cetera Advisor Networks LLC. Cryptocurrencies and other Blockchain-related non-securities products cannot be recommended, offered, or held by the firm.

For a comprehensive review of your personal situation, always consult with a tax or legal advisor. Neither Cetera Advisor Networks LLC nor any of its representatives may give legal or tax advice.

Generally, a donor-advised fund is a separately identified fund or account that is maintained and operated by a section 501(c)(3) organization, which is called a sponsoring organization. Each account is composed of contributions made by individual donors. Once the donor makes the contribution, the organization has legal control over it. However, the donor, or the donor's representative, retains advisory privileges with respect to the distribution of funds and the investment of assets in the account. Donors take a tax deduction for all contributions at the time they are made, even though the money may not be dispersed to a charity until much later.

The cost and availability of life insurance depend on factors such as age, health, and the type and amount of insurance purchased. Before implementing a strategy involving life insurance, it would be prudent to make sure that you are insurable by having the policy approved. As with most financial decisions, there are expenses associated with the purchase of life insurance. Policies commonly have mortality and expense charges. In addition, if a policy is surrendered prematurely, there may be surrender charges and income tax implications.

Steve Short is not affiliated or registered with Cetera Advisor Networks LLC. Any information provided by this individual is in no way related to Cetera Advisor Networks LLC or its registered representatives.

Registered branch address: 1890 Maine St., Quincy, IL 62301